GLORY DAYS

The History of New Port Richey, Florida

Written by

Brian Schmit

Cover Photo: Taken at the Hacienda Hotel, New Port Richey Press, February 3rd, 1928. Left to right: Marjorie Sims, Flora Zabelle, Frances Ring, Gene Sarazen, Christine Mangasarian, George Sims, Mary Sarazen, Earl Benham. Courtesy of the West Pasco Historical Society

All Photos courtesy of West Pasco Historical Society and Jeff Miller unless otherwise noted.

ISBN: 978-1-942634-79-9

Printed in the United States of America

Digital Publishing of Florida, Inc.
www.digitaldata-corp.com

Acknowledgements

I would like to express my sincerest gratitude to all the people who have contributed to the making of this book. I thank the members of the West Pasco Historical Society who have put in countless volunteer hours to maintain the history of our wonderful community. First among them is Jeff Miller, whose work in chronicling the area's history through an extraordinary collection of photographs and information is unparalleled. I also want to thank all those citizens who took the time to tell me the stories of their heritage and their own personal recollections that make up the vibrant tapestry of New Port Richey. Finally, I am grateful for all my many friends and family for their continued support in my efforts to interpret and preserve our history.

A great deal of my research came from the extensive collection of newspaper articles held by the West Pasco Historical Society.

GLORY DAYS

The History of New Port Richey, Florida

TABLE OF CONTENTS

Glory Days

The History of New Port Richey, Florida

Introduction

In October of 2015, the City of New Port Richey decided to open its historic hotel, the Hacienda, to another round of tours. The beautiful 1920s era hotel was once the winter home of some of the most famous people in the country. Eighty years had passed since its glory days of welcoming celebrities to the whimsical hotel nestled along the banks of the meandering Cotee River. The once grandiose building had been boarded up for nearly a decade, and the thrill of the nation's aristocrats walking the New Port Richey streets was nothing more than a distant memory. However, thanks to a million dollar grant from the State of Florida, and a calculated investment by the city, the Hacienda Hotel was about to undergo a historic restoration returning it to its majestic days of the roaring twenties. A time when New Port Richey was on the cusp of becoming the "Hollywood of the East."

There was plenty of excitement on the day of the tours. My wife Marjie and I wanted to get there early to make sure we had a spot for one of the guided tours. Since arriving in New Port Richey from Minnesota eleven years ago, we had heard rumors that New Port Richey had an incredible history. This history has been largely forgotten and most considered this as little more than a nondescript impoverished area bypassed by the congestion of the giant albatross of US Highway 19. Stories of luxurious parties with prohibition era gangsters operating in the shadows were exciting to imagine. The local population tossed around names like Al Capone, Babe Ruth, Irving

1

Berlin, Gloria Swanson, and Charlie Chaplin, as people who frequented the Hacienda. In our eyes, all that amazing history seemed to be locked away in the pink stucco palace whose doors were about to come unchained for us to explore its rich contents. As we pulled up to the Mediterranean style building next door to Sims Park, we saw a couple hundred people already formed in lines awaiting their chance to peek inside the historic walls.

Members of the historical society, city administrators, and members of a group called *Friends of the Hacienda* led the tours. The group had a table set up out front where they sold memberships. I bought a membership to support the cause but also because the black t-shirt that came with it was pretty cool looking. After getting our name on a list, we started snooping around the area and noticed a sign erected in front of the building.

HACIENDA HOTEL RENOVATION PROJECT
Built 1927 – Restored 2015
CITY OF NEW PORT RICHEY

The sign listed the architects that were undertaking the restoration. One was a local company out of Tampa (Atelier AEC Inc.) and the other firm was Bender and Associates out of Key West. I overheard someone in the crowd remark that one of the architects was leading a tour. I hoped he'd be our guide.

After about twenty minutes, our group was called forward and introduced to our guide. John was about sixty years old with a gray mustache and he wore sandals. Not the architect we were hoping for, but a friendly guy nonetheless. He started off by quizzing us on what we already knew about the celebrities who stayed at the Hacienda. People in our tour group rattled off several famous names. It seemed everyone who was anyone was here during the city's early years in the 1920s and 30s. I glanced over at my wife with my eyebrows raised. She seemed equally as excited by the intriguing prospects of the tour. John tried to stump us by asking us about a famous golfer who not only stayed at the Hacienda but also built a home along the river.

"Does anyone know who the first winner of all four major golf championships was?" I was all over this one. "Gene Sarazen," I proudly exclaimed. I cheated, however, having read it in a brochure just minutes earlier. "That's right," John responded with a little of his thunder taken. But then he recovered well, "he also invented the sand wedge right down the street!" As an avid golfer who has been in many sand traps, I felt a kindred spirit to Sarazen. With the quiz portion of the tour now over, John turned and motioned us to follow him.

As we circled the outside of the building, John explained all the changes that were made to the structure since 1927. The biggest being that the main entrance was moved from the east side, facing the street, to the north side, facing the park. He explained how everything would be changed back to its original form, which included eliminating the entire lobby area that was added on to the new entrance during the 1970s. When we entered the lobby, there were old pictures of the Hacienda on display. Looking at the pictures and then at the lobby, you could get a good sense of how it used to look and how it will look again. Back in the 1920s, three beautiful masonry arches lead to a huge patio overlooking the park. The Friends of the Hacienda displayed an old hotel brochure on an easel that proclaimed the iconic hotel as "A bit of old Spain amid the palms." The picture below the catchy slogan showed the expansive patio and Mediterranean arches as a splendid tropical oasis surrounded by whimsical palms. It's a shame that it had been covered up with a makeshift lobby.

The tour moved through the building with John showing us what it once was and what it soon will be after the restoration. All very interesting, but my wife and I were waiting for the juicy stuff. Where's the sex, drugs, and rock and roll, or at least big band music? Then, as if on cue, we saw a paper sign taped to the back stairway of the kitchen. In black marker, the sign read "Bordello" and had an arrow pointing up the stairs. Now there's something you don't see every day. Well, at least my wife and I don't anyway. John led the group up the narrow staircase and into a hallway with three rooms on both sides. We peered into the small rooms that were big enough to fit one bed and little else. Then again, if the rooms were used for what the sign indicated, that was all that was required. John told us the only way to get in or out of the bordello was through the kitchen or down the stairs from the second floor. The rooms were roped off, but it didn't stop every person in the group from looking wide-eyed into the rooms as if the scandalous acts were actually taking place right then and there.

"There's one other way that some mischievous gentlemen might have snuck their way into the bordello," John said with every head turning towards him. "They could have come in through the secret tunnel that went out to the river." The crowd paused in silence, waiting for more information. I was also in disbelief, because as cool as that sounded, I had to wonder about a tunnel in a town that was barely above sea level. Then John continued, "Originally I was surprised when the tunnel went in a northwesterly direction under the park, and not a southwesterly direction towards the bridge where men could enter the tunnel unseen. But in 1927 there was a different bridge that crossed the river, and that bridge was located in the direction of the tunnel." I looked over to my wife to see what her reaction was and she seemed to be hooked. Who wouldn't be interested in a story of perfidious men sneaking through secret tunnels to a back room bordello? With everyone's curiosity piqued, John continued. "Not only that, but remember the Hacienda was built during prohibition. The tunnel was a perfect way for bootleggers like Capone to smuggle booze in and out of the hotel from the river." This tour was getting more and more interesting. I was amazed a place like this even existed in our little town. I couldn't wait to see the tunnel, but instead of leading us down to the basement, John led us up the stairs to the second floor.

It was at that moment, reflecting back on all the fascinating things from the first floor, that I determined that a book had to be written about all the crazy things that happened in such an unlikely place far off Florida's beaten paths. But that was only the beginning. On the second floor were most of the fifty guest rooms. The rooms were small by today's standards. The upstairs was not nearly as extravagant as the main floor. More functional than glamorous. Because of this, John whisked us along through the hallways from one side of the hotel to the other. When we reached a corner room, John stopped and proclaimed before going in, "This is my favorite room." It was a two-room suite with a winding staircase off the back wall. "This room was built specifically for Gloria Swanson, one of the biggest silent picture stars of the time!" John was very excited about Gloria Swanson spending time in this room. I had recognized the name but did not know specifically who she was. Telling us about her great beauty and popularity, John led us to the stairway. "This staircase goes up to the tower that rises high above the Hacienda. Gloria loved to sit in her private tower, watch the sun set in the evenings, and enjoy the tropical breezes coming off the Gulf."

As cool as the tower was, there was also a sad story involving Gloria's tower. John told us that one of the young girls from the bordello had hanged herself in the tower after Gloria returned to Hollywood. Her body could be seen by the entire town, hanging in the tower. It was a haunting thought of the poor girl swaying back and forth in the wind. John knew of business owners around town that claim to see the ghost of the girl peering down from the tower then slowly vanishing in the breeze. Someone in the group asked John if they knew why she hanged herself. John sighed and headed towards the door. "Come with me; there's more to the story." Somehow, I knew there would be.

We walked down to the other end of the hotel where there was another nice room, similar to Gloria's suite. This time, instead of its own private tower, the suite had a beautiful sunroom facing south with lots of windows to capture the Florida sun. "This was the room used by Joseph Kennedy," John explained. Then it hit me. That is where I knew the name, Gloria Swanson. I had recently watched a movie about the Kennedy Family in general, and Joseph Kennedy in particular. Gloria Swanson was the mistress of Joe Kennedy. It was one of those affairs of the rich and famous that everyone knew about, but nobody spoke about. Both of them were married, but both liked to wander. Supposedly Joe's wife, Rose, was a wholesome and good woman with conservative Catholic values. But this buttoned-up stance did not satisfy the playboy Kennedy who was not above frolicking with the alluring Gloria Swanson.

Here is where John's story about the girl's death resumed. It turns out the young lady was a big fan of Gloria Swanson, having seen her in the movies shown at the Palms Theatre down the street. One evening she got up the nerve to approach Ms. Swanson for an autograph when Gloria and Joe were having dinner in the hotel's restaurant. As the girl approached the table, Gloria noticed that Joe's eyes were checking out the pretty and scantily clad girl, from her perky top to her well-shaped bottom. This was too much for Gloria who was not going to be upstaged by another woman, especially in front of her lover. John told us, "Gloria ripped into her pretty good. She called the shocked girl a worthless little whore and made a scene in front of the entire restaurant. The girl went running away in tears, humiliated by someone she had idolized." Apparently, the ordeal had traumatized the girl to the degree that she became distraught. She was ashamed of who she had become and devastated over her sins being uncovered in front of everyone. The day after Gloria Swanson checked out of the Hacienda, the girl snuck into her room, climbed the tower stairs, and took her own life.

After viewing that last room, John thanked us for coming to the Hacienda tours, and we thanked John for all the stories and showing us around. More than satisfied with the tour, we walked down the steps and back into the light of the day. As we walked back to our car, Marjie and I talked about what it must have been like to live in New Port Richey during the Roaring Twenties with all the celebrities walking the streets. Marjie asked me how much of what we heard was true. I was not sure, but if even half of it were, it would make for an entertaining story.

In the weeks that followed, I went about doing some preliminary research. To my astonishment, the story of a Roaring Twenties haven for the famous was even better than I imagined. Among the celebrities who spent time in New Port Richey were Academy Award-winning movie stars, directors, and producers, Grammy-winning singers, composers and musicians, best-selling authors, famous attorneys, world-class athletes, some of the wealthiest men in the world, and a man who walked on the moon. Most notable, however, were the celebrities who actually owned homes in New Port Richey and contributed to the community. Thomas Meighan, who built a mansion on the Cotee River, was one of the most sought after leading men in motion pictures during the 1920s. Gene Sarazen was Meighan's neighbor in New Port Richey and ranks as one of the top ten greatest golfers of all time. Years later, legendary country music singer Johnny Cash and his wife June Carter inherited a house on the river where they spent many sultry days fishing the bayous of the Gulf. The fact that all these people came together in a place like New Port Richey was astonishing. The story of a celebrity boomtown during the 1920s is a wonderful slice of time in American pop culture.

This book will focus on telling the true story of what occurred in the early years of New Port Richey. What actually happened in this little Florida town was magical. For a few short years, the founding fathers of New Port Richey made a valiant effort at starting a motion picture colony. The story of how New Port Richey came to the brink of fame and fortune was nothing less than remarkable. They referred to their city as the "Hollywood of the East," and seemingly made all the right moves. The dreams of the fledgling city came to a perilous end however, when the stock market crashed on October 29th, 1929. But this is not a story about what might have been; it is the story of what was, New Port Richey's glory days.

1

Captain Richey

There have been many inhabitants of the land along the Gulf Coast of Florida. Prior to European exploration of the area, the native population consisted of a peaceful group of farmers and fishermen known as the Tocobaga. The main Tocobaga village rested on the northern shores of Tampa Bay where a giant sacred mound was constructed. The mound is made up of soil along with bones and shells that were discarded refuse from the Tocobaga diet of wildlife and seafood. The Tocobaga built a structure on the top of the mound used either for religious ceremonies or as a residence for the chief. That mound is preserved today at Philippi Park in the city of Safety Harbor, north of Tampa Bay. In the city of Port Richey, near the mouth of the Pithlachascotee River, is a similar but smaller ceremonial mound of earth and shells. At this location, another tribe of the Tocobaga lived. These indigenous people, who had been in the area for more than a thousand years, were here when Spanish explorers invaded their lands in the sixteenth century. Ponce De Leon arrived in Tampa Bay in 1521, Panfilo De Narvaez in 1528, and Hernando De Soto in 1539. Whether by warfare with the Europeans or a by a deadly outbreak of a disease like smallpox, the Tocobaga had disappeared by the time Americans expanded southward into Florida.

By the nineteenth century, the Seminole Indians, a diverse tribe made up of runaway slaves, Spaniards, and migrating Creek Indians from Georgia, had spread across Florida. General Andrew Jackson drove the Seminoles from the northern regions of the state when they had posed a problem of looting Georgia farmers. The Seminoles remained entrenched deep in the natural refuge of Florida swamps when the U.S. Army pursued them as part of the Indian Removal Act. In 1824, Fort Brooke was established in Tampa to aid in the Seminole Indian Wars. The fort brought Americans south into the relatively untouched region for the first time. One commanding officer stationed at Fort Brooke was future president Zachary Taylor.

For years, the area northwest of Tampa Bay, known then as Hickory Hammock, remained relatively unpopulated. Among the people who made their way to the area north and south of the Anclote River before the Civil War, were a couple of government surveyors named Samuel Hope and Peter Baillie. Legend has it that while serving at Fort Brooke during the Civil War, Samuel Hope was called upon when a group of Confederate soldiers and their slaves ran off from the fort into the area of Hickory Hammock. It was Hope that was sent to track them down and eventually hang them for desertion.

Both Samuel Hope and P.K. Baillie brought their families back to the area after the Civil War was over. The parcel of high ground along the Gulf is today called Bailey's Bluff. There is an amusing legend about how Baillie became the owner of the land.

P.K. Baillie was a government surveyor assigned to Florida's west coast after the Civil War. While surveying the west coast, Baillie came across the Tocobaga Indian village along the north end of Tampa Bay. The chief of the tribe was in great grief because his only son was stricken with malaria and on his deathbed. Baillie administered quinine to the boy, which broke his fever and restored his health. According to P.K. Baillie's grandson David, so grateful was the chief, he took Baillie to a high mound, from which one could see for miles in all directions, and with a sweep of his arm he gave the entire area to his benefactor. The Chief slit his palm with a knife and signed a parchment legally giving the land to Baillie. Years later the government, which had recorded the land transaction, paid each of the Baillie heirs one hundred dollars to sign a release of the land.

The families of Peter Baillie and Samuel Hope were among the first settlers of the area. Yet, it was another man whose name was officially attached to the cities of Port Richey and New Port Richey; Aaron McLaughlin Richey hailed from St. Joseph, Missouri, the designated starting point for pioneers and wagon trains heading into the western frontier. It was there that Richey took a job as a trail hand on a wagon train bound for Sacramento. This adventurous spirit of forging into new lands and new opportunities would lead Richey to blaze a trail of his own, this time into the tropical wilderness of the Florida Gulf coast.

In the 1800s, Florida was sparsely populated. This was partly due to the challenging summer climate, and partly due to unrest with the Seminole Indians. In an effort to encourage settlers to move south, The United States government enacted the Armed Occupation Act of 1842. This offered 160 acres to anyone willing to build a home on the property and live there at least five years. This act opened up the new frontier of Florida and brought adventurous souls south. In 1883, Hamilton Disston bought four million acres in western Florida for 25 cents an acre. With Disston taking the lead, other investors began looking for their opportunity to buy cheap and sell high. Disston's improvements of Florida's infrastructure lead to, among other things, the formation of the town of Tarpon Springs. Much like the western migration of the mid-1800s, Florida was at the beginning stages of a land boom. It was under these circumstances that A. M. Richey brought his wife and three children to look for opportunities in Florida.

The Richeys began their new Florida life in Brooksville, where they met James W. Clark, the town's butcher. Clark told Richey about some property he owned, in a place called Hopeville along the Pithlachascotee River. Clark, also a cattle rancher, originally had come to the area after continually finding his herd wandering south each year. Eventually, Clark decided to follow the cattle's lead and just move to the area himself. His wife, Fanny Hope, was already familiar with the area. Fanny was the daughter of David Hope and Frances Pyles. The Hope family had been in Hickory Hammock since the Civil War. Samuel Hope had told his uncle, David Hope, about the area and the family soon began mining salt from the nearby springs. The salt works supplied the Confederate Army with salt during the Civil War. David Hope was married to Frances Pyles whose family has the distinction of being one of the first British families to live in St. Augustine, Florida. The Pyles had moved to St. Augustine in 1762, the first year in which the British took control of Florida from the Spanish.

The Clark family raised cattle and grew citrus fruits on their land. They were the first permanent settlers to the area, and in 1878, James W. Clark became the postmaster of the Hopeville post office. With no deputies in the area and few neighbors within miles, settlers were pretty much on their own to ward off any attacks. Hopeville was ripe for cattle rustlers and bandits. After several years of living in Hopeville, the Clarks briefly returned to Brooksville when a baby was due to be born and they became worried for their family's safety.

Many times during the early years in the area, the Clark family was threatened by things other than the elements. Cattle thieves were among the worst. Clark witnessed a murder by one of the rustlers ... fearing for his life.
Francis Clark Mallett, James Clark granddaughter

Clark wanted to return to the home he had left behind, but he was concerned about the safety of his wife and five children. Feeling it would be safer if other families moved into the area, Clark brought Richey to the banks of the beautiful Pithlachascotee River in 1881. Upon seeing the land, Richey knew that this was the opportunity he had been searching for. Clark told Richey about another settler named Felix Sowers who owned land at the mouth of the river and was looking to move back to his home in Atlanta. Richey was able to buy Sowers' house and orange grove along with seventy-six acres that Sowers had purchased from the government.

Life was quite different for the Richey family living in Florida for the first time. One reason Richey chose to bring his family to Florida was his belief that the warm climate and fresh sea air from the Gulf would help his wife who had been sickly over the years.

Unfortunately, any benefits of the weather were offset by the isolated surroundings of the Richey homestead.

The most lonesome years of my life… for sometimes it was three months at a time that mother and I did not see a woman. Mrs. Malcolm Hill was the other woman in that section, and she lived some distance away.

Maggie Richey, A.M. Richey daughter

The area was bountiful with fish and wild game and the family was well fed. The challenge was that the closest connection to the modern world was the small town of Tarpon Springs some ten miles down the coast. Richey soon tired of traveling through the thicket on horseback for supplies in Tarpon Springs, and he realized that it would be easier to get around on the water. He made plans to purchase a schooner from a ship builder in Cedar Key. When asked for the name of the port that the schooner would be registered, Richey responded by calling his home *Port Richey*. From that point on A.M. Richey would be known as Captain Richey, and the place where he lived was Port Richey. The name Port Richey soon replaced the earlier name of Hopeville.

With the schooner, Captain Richey was able to supply other settlers in the area with goods he sold out of a small store in his home. Soon after, in 1884, he established a post office in his home and became the first postmaster of Port Richey. Riders on horseback, a slower version of the pony express, delivered the mail. The riders took the mail from Brooksville to Tarpon Springs and all areas between. The Richey family lived in their home for eight years before Captain Richey experienced heart problems. His poor health forced the family to move to Tarpon Springs where the only doctor in the area resided. When Richey left his home in Port Richey, the post office location was transferred to the home of James W. Clark. Having already served as a postmaster for the earlier town of Hopeville, Clark had no problem maintaining those duties until his death. As for A. M. Richey, he managed to stay healthy enough to become mayor of Tarpon Springs.

The house of Aaron McLaughlin Richey

The Richey family and friends by the Pithlachascotee River, 1892

James and Frances Clark

Residence of Mr. J. W. Clark, Sr., on bank of Cootee River.

The Clark House on the Cotee River

2

New Port Richey

Soon the entire area around the Pithlachascotee River became known as Port Richey but it remained sparsely inhabited due to the remoteness and the dense growth of palmettos, palms, cypress, oak and longleaf pine. Pioneers who braved the conditions and followed the families of Hope, Clark, and Richey to the Port Richey area include the families of Nicks, Hill, Stevenson, Miller, Brown, Luikart, and Mitchell. The landscape would change beginning in 1904 when a Georgia corporation owned by five wealthy men, all with their last names beginning with the letter "A," opened the Aripeka Saw Mills, just north of Port Richey. A little boom town rose up from the 1500 workers that came to cut the timber pines, and was known as "Five A," or more commonly as "Fivay." The sawmill was quite productive at clearing the tall pine in what is today western Pasco County. Like the California gold rush, the Florida timber industry was a volatile business. When the gold ran out in San Francisco, the miners left in droves. The same thing happened to Fivay when the land was cleared of timber. As quickly as the little mill town was built, it was dismantled and a virtual ghost town remained.

The boilers of the mill were never cold, a day and night shift kept the Mill in constant operation. Millions of feet were cut from the maiden forest and shipped to the northern and southern markets. The timber supply was finally exhausted, a town without a payroll, abandoned.

J.A. Hendley, early settler

In 1911, the land was sold to Peter Weeks, who formed the Port Richey Company to develop the newly cleared land. The prime spot for development became the area previously known as Hickory Hammock surrounding a small lake near the banks of the Pithlachascotee River. The area was just up the river from where the Clarks first settled in Port Richey. The name Pithlachascotee comes from a Seminole Indian term meaning "hacked out canoe." The locals were now shortening the name of the river to the "Cootee" and eventually the "Cotee."

What made the cleared land especially appealing was the presence of a pristine lake, just two hundred yards from the Cotee River. Formed by a large and rounded sinkhole, Orange Lake was originally called Blue Sink. The Port Richey Company hired W.E. Guilford to manage their affairs in the area. Guilford laid out a plat map for the future town on a grid of north/south and east/west streets. This planned community contained hundreds of lots marked by white stakes ready for sale. What was once a dense forest was now a community brimming with potential and ready for business.

The Port Richey Company opened an office in Tampa where they hoped to attract buyers from the northern states looking to invest in Florida land. Tampa had become a destination point thanks to Henry Plant who bought up southern rail companies after the civil war and expanded their reach into Florida and to Tampa. Plant had a vast empire of boats, trains, and hotels that helped an expanding population spend their vacation money in sunny Florida. He was in a friendly competition for northern travelers with fellow railroad tycoon Henry Flagler, whose rail lines ran along the Atlantic coast of Florida. When Flagler built the luxurious Ponce De Leon Hotel in St. Augustine, Plant responded by building the equally impressive Tampa Bay Hotel. With great pride, Plant invited his rival to spend a weekend at his newly finished hotel in Tampa. To which Flagler responded tongue in cheek, "Where's Tampa?" Plant, rising to the challenge of wits, advised his competitor to "just follow the crowds."

For many people looking to buy Florida land, the Tampa Hotel was their point of entry. It was for this reason the Port Richey Company had their office in Tampa near the hotel. W.E. Guilford placed numerous advertisements in the northern newspapers to attract investors, but had little luck so far. That was until Fred Sass of Missouri happened upon the Port Richey Company in 1912.

We left the thermometer at Kansas City registering a temperature of five degrees below zero. After putting up at the Tampa Hotel... and about three weeks search for the Promised Land, we heard of the Port Richey Company.

Fred Sass

Mr. Guilford drove Fred and Ollie Sass out to the Port Richey land on an old dirt road once used by soldiers from Fort Brooke in Tampa. When they arrived in Port Richey, there were only a few buildings in town, owned mostly by those connected with the land company. One building that caught the Sass's attention was a half-finished hotel near Orange Lake. After Guilford had taken them on a boat ride down the Cotee, Fred Sass was delighted with what he saw and quickly arranged to buy the hotel. Although the area had been mostly cleared of vegetation by the sawmill, it was still pretty rough in places. In fact, standing on the porch of the hotel, you could not see Orange Lake which was less than thirty yards away.

The Sass Hotel became a fixture in the growing community. Mrs. Sass was the first woman to live in the newly developed area, and gained a reputation as a good cook and hostess. Especially popular was her fish fry. Community involvement improved when Mrs. Sass organized the "Port Richey Settlers Benefit Club," for which she hosted monthly dinners that cost 35 cents a plate. Fred Sass entertained guests at the inn by feeding a nine-foot alligator in Orange Lake. The gator, who was named Jack, would swim up to the dock when Fred pounded a stick against the piling. Fred stuck a piece of meat to the end of the stick, then Jack lunged out of the water snapping it up in its massive jaws to the delight of the travelers. Later, there was a great deal of controversy among the residents of New Port Richey when Jack grew too big for everyone's comfort.

One of the early residents who took an interest in growing the town was Gerben DeVries, who came down with his family from Michigan. He arrived with his wife Ellen, who became instrumental in her own right, leading a women's club. Gerben came to Florida on doctor's orders to recuperate after a long bout of malaria. They built a little two-room house a couple of blocks from the lake on Central Avenue. However most of the streets that ran east and west were named after states. Streets that ran north and south were named after Presidents in order from George Washington to James K. Polk.

Gerben DeVries took a job with the Port Richey Land Company and was quite content with living in the friendly little town. Yet he saw the need for improvement.

For food supplies, outside of what we shot in the woods or caught in the river and lakes, we depended on the pantry in the Sass Hotel and the post office store at Port Richey.

Gerben DeVries

It was difficult to get the mail from Port Richey since there were no direct roads between the cities. The land between the towns was called the "Devil's Wood Yard" because of the thick growth of trees and underbrush. The best route to Port Richey was by rowboat down the Cotee River. One of Gerben's jobs was to get the mail for the Port Richey Land Office and others in the town. Gerben would make the best of it and drop in a fish line as he rowed along.

I remember one day I caught 36 trout and jack fish trawling to Port Richey after the mail. Generally, the one who went got the mail for the rest of the bunch. He was also expected to bring back two fish for each letter. If there were a dozen letters it was up to him to catch 24 fish. As we increased in population, we tired of this.

Gerben DeVries

20

The logical solution was to get a post office of their own so that the mail could be delivered directly to them. Gerben DeVries started two petitions. One to bring a post office and another to make him postmaster. There were 80 names on each petition that included everyone in the surrounding area. Since the land company had done quite a lot of advertising in northern cities, they didn't want to change the name of Port Richey, which they worked so hard to establish. They decided to call their post office "Newport Richey." Later, they came to find out that there already was a town called Newport Florida. Since there was some worry that it would cause confusion, the name was changed slightly to New Port Richey.

In 1915, Gerben DeVries received his commission, and the post office was opened in the land office building. The post office had fifteen small wooden "pigeon holes" where incoming mail could be put in alphabetical order to be picked up by the townspeople. Gerben was paid twenty-five dollars a month for his position as postmaster. The mail arrived each day by horseback stopping at Port Richey and New Port Richey along the way. There was no more need for Gerben to row his boat to get the mail, but the fishing remained the same.

Besides the post office, New Port Richey got another boost when rail service was extended from Elfers to New Port Richey. For a while, the closest any railway service came to New Port Richey was Tarpon Springs. The Orange Belt Line started in Sanford, went southwest to Tarpon Springs then finished in St. Petersburg. Interestingly, the city of St. Petersburg took its name from the hometown of the railroad tycoon who built the line, Peter Demens of St. Petersburg, Russia. John Williams, the developer of the city, wanted to name it after his hometown of Detroit, but lost when drawing straws with Demens for naming rights.

In 1913 it was the Tampa and Gulf Coast Railroad Company, affectionately called the "Tug and Grunt" that originally brought the line to Elfers. The railroad came to Elfers with the support of the Elfers Citrus Growers Association who needed transportation for their products and workers. With the continued growth of New Port Richey, the railroad extended another six miles across the Cotee River and into downtown in 1914. New Port Richey was the last stop heading north, so the train had to turn around at the railway hub south of Elfers and back up some six miles into the station. The Tug and Grunt arrived twice daily and the whole town would turn out to greet the passengers.

The railroad connected the city of New Port Richey with the mainstream population of Tampa, and more importantly energized the city to believe that it was headed towards growth and prosperity. In this manner, the cities of New Port Richey and Port Richey began to drift apart. Port Richey, without a railroad stop, remained disconnected from the thriving Tampa Bay area and had little inclination to change. Conversely, New Port Richey had their city laid out for growth, and open for business. Another hotel called the Grand Rapids Inn was built near the Sass Hotel. It quickly became too small and had to build an addition, reorganized as the Hotel Newport. Hotel space was important to the Port Richey Company (which kept its name despite the town it was building now being referred to as New Port Richey), which was hard at work bringing people to town for visits. In New Port Richey, there was a sense of optimism that the town was on the verge of something special. Meanwhile, the neighboring city of Port Richey was perfectly content to remain unencumbered by the outside world and to continue living a laid-back lifestyle.

In January of 1916, a newspaper called the New Port Richey Post published its first edition, another stepping-stone of the town's evolution. The newspaper proudly printed the news of two more improvements; the opening of the New Port Richey Drug Store and Soda Fountain.

The post office is located in the drug store quarters, and in other sections of the building is located the dry goods store of W.H. Valentine, the meat market of J.W. Clark, and on the second floor may be found W.A. Casey's barbershop, Dr. Posey's office and other items of interest.

New Port Richey Post

A two story school was built on Main Street in 1915. There were four other schools in the area, one in Port Richey, one in Elfers, one in an area known as Seven Springs on the Anclote River, and one called the Cootie School, just east of town. Business leaders purchased the first fire truck for the city in 1917. It was a Ford Model T heavy duty fire truck with a water tank but no pumper. At first, there were few cars in New Port Richey, mostly horses and oxen. Automobiles became common as a means for northern tourists and investors to get to Florida. Ford introduced its popular Model T in 1908 at the cost of $825, just out of reach of the average American. However, by 1912 the price had dropped to $575, making it possible for the middle class to own cars.

With the emergence of the automobile, suitable roadways were the next challenge for travelers. Only ten percent of U.S. roads were surfaced in 1914. Dirt roads that were overused became laden with holes that took their toll on the stiff automobiles, leading to numerous breakdowns alongside the roads. There was a movement to build a national highway from the far north to the far south. With the federal government not wanting to commit funds, the task fell on the states. The Dixie Highway Association formed with two delegates from each state. Each state was responsible for their portion. The Florida state highway system began in 1915 to manage this directive. There were two routes of the Dixie Highway. One running from Detroit to Miami and the other from Chicago to Naples. There were cross-over highways between the two routes, in Knoxville and Atlanta. Construction of the interstate highway began in 1915 and was finished in 1927.

Tourists now had the ability to travel on a well-maintained road with a direct route to Florida. Relief from the cold winters of the north was only a matter of a few days' car ride. Travelers headed south were often called "tin can tourists" as they camped along the Dixie Highway and ate their meals out of tin cans. In Florida, the states passed the responsibility of paving the Dixie Highway to the local communities that benefited from the highway. When it came New Port Richey's turn to complete their portion of the highway, they poured crushed rock dredged from the Cotee River onto Grand Boulevard. Grand Boulevard from Port Richey to Elfers became part of the Dixie Highway system, bringing numerous travelers right through the heart of the fledgling city.

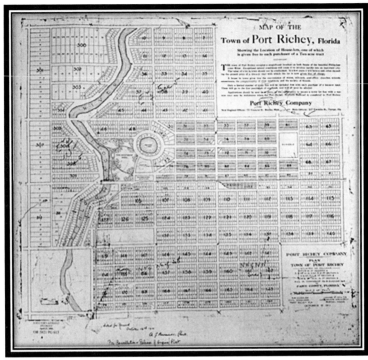

City grid laid out by the Port Richey Company

Sass Hotel, New Port Richey

Port Richey Land Office. Mike Broersma and Fred Rowan

New Port Richey Train Depot

3

Founding Fathers

For all the growth that New Port Richey was experiencing with the arrival of the Tug and Grunt railroad and the Dixie Highway, the little town was still woven into the fabric of the rural countryside. Fencing laws were adopted throughout the country and the state, but not yet in New Port Richey. Cattle and hogs routinely clogged the dirt streets and occasionally even made their way through the front door of downtown businesses. Florida had long been a state of *crackers*. The name *crackers* originated from ranchers who cracked their whips when herding their cattle. With few cities and wide open acreage, it was unnecessary for ranchers to fence in their grazing areas. Cattle and other livestock were allowed to roam free, often miles from their homestead.

New Port Richey might have remained a sleepy country town if not for the arrival of a keen businessman. George Sims purchased the Port Richey Company and 14,000 acres of land along the Cotee River in 1916. Upon their arrival, George and Marjorie Sims stayed at the Sass Hotel where they started getting accustomed to their back-to-nature life. George, who was used to the fast pace of his hometown of Detroit, Michigan and his summer retreat of Great Neck, New York, got right to work.

In fact, I did not get my first glimpse of the river until several days after my arrival, being busy at the office of the Port Richey Company; but Mrs. Sims amused herself running a small motor boat up and down the river. One day she announced that she would like to have a winter home here.

George Sims

With plenty of choices of where to build their bungalow, George and Marjorie had their first major disagreement. George wanted to live in town on the circle drive around Orange Lake, Marjorie wanted to live in the country. George later remarked in the sarcastic manner that many husbands do after a squabble with their wives.

We argued the matter for several days and finally compromised by building the bungalow where she wanted it.

George Sims

Once established, Sims began selling lots to families from Michigan who were looking to move to Florida and get into the citrus business that was prospering in neighboring Elfers. The turpentine and lumber industries were also thriving, and Sims used them for recruitment as well. The Port Richey Land Company sold land for $50 per acre in 1916. City lots 50' X 150' ran between $50 and $250 depending on proximity to water, downtown, and roads. Visitors to New Port Richey could look upon about a square mile of home sites marked with white painted posts.

The best luck George Sims had was selling land to wealthy New Yorkers looking for a winter home in Florida. Sims was part of a summer theater colony outside Manhattan in the community of Great Neck, on Long Island. With the Florida land boom, many residents of Great Neck were looking to make a move to Florida for the winter months. The motion picture industry, which began in northern cities like New York and Chicago, was also looking to warm weather climates like Florida and California to film during the winter months. Hollywood was starting to establish itself as the primary location of the country's movie industry. Travel to the west coast was an issue in the 1920s, and the possibility of an east coast movie production location was a real possibility. George Sims figured that New Port Richey had as good a shot as any city of becoming the "Hollywood of the East."

Florida had plenty of suitors for the movie business. Jacksonville, Miami, and Tampa were all vying for the business. Of the three Florida cities, Jacksonville had the upper hand. They were able to attract the Kalem Production Company, which introduced a budding silent screen star named Oliver Hardy. Yet with each passing year, California drew more and more film producers to the west coast. Florida posed two challenges for the film industry. First, the high humidity was uncomfortable to work in, but also made the actor's makeup run and smudge. The second challenge was economics. Florida did not have the political support that could give the production companies tax relief and monetary incentive to move to the state. People were pouring into Florida with the land boom, but it was just too early to expect the economic infrastructure to be in place to support the film industry. Despite these disadvantages, there was enough activity and growth in Florida to draw interest from production companies.

For the town of New Port Richey to be successful it had to be more than a glorified resort community. It needed a civic foundation to provide the infrastructure of government including services to the community. To this end, the citizens of New Port Richey were very fortunate when 75-year-old Dr. Elroy Avery decided to reside in their little city. Dr. Avery was a Civitan of the highest order, which was what the young town needed. In his career as a public servant, Dr. Avery was a teacher, principal, and a superintendent. He served two enlistments in the Union Army during the Civil War. At the University of Michigan, he earned a Masters of Philosophy, along with three honorary Doctoral degrees. Dr. Avery served on the Cleveland City Council and as a member of the Ohio State Senate. He wrote numerous textbooks on history, physics, and chemistry. He brought those books along with a collection of over a thousand books with him to New Port Richey, which he used to start the city's first Library and Historical Society. The library was originally located in the newly built Snell Building on Main Street. The Avery Library was one of the finest in the state. As a 32nd degree Free Mason and a Knight Templar, Dr. Avery was a shining example of a benevolent citizen. He would come to be known as the "Grand Old Man of New Port Richey."

The town continued to move forward at a rapid pace. Warren Burns, an industrialist from New York City, and his brother Clyde, of Chicago, arrived in New Port Richey for the purpose of building an electric company. The Gulf Utility Company was built with $120,000, using coal fired steam engines and began supplying power to the city in 1919. The new electric company installed electrical lines on poles throughout New Port Richey. Suddenly the town was lit up by the glow of Edison's incandescent light bulbs. The Gulf Utility Company charged residents 18 cents per kilowatt-hour to have light bulbs replace the oil lamps in their homes. Electrical service was available from 5:00 a.m. until 11:00 p.m. daily. The plant was located next to the Tug and Grunt railway, where it rounded the bend entering the city. The railway cars loaded with coal for the plant, stopped short of the train station to unload the coal, before continuing the final quarter mile to pick up passengers. Simultaneous to building the electrical plant, Warren Burns also constructed an ice making facility.

Having adopted James Watt's steam engine, and Thomas Edison's light bulbs, New Port Richey welcomed Alexander Graham Bell's telephones that same year. As a side note, Thomas Watson, the man at the other end of the historic first phone call, would one day reside in New Port Richey. Technology had its grip on the city, and it was full steam ahead. A novelty for such a small town, telephones soon connected homes and businesses throughout the city. The local newspaper proudly printed their phone number in the Christmas Day edition.

The telephone number of the Port Richey Press is 120-0. One long and two short rings will call us up on the local line.

Port Richey Press, 1919

30

George Sims constructed the town's first brick building on the corner of Main and Grand. At this location, the Port Richey Company was ideally situated in the heart of the city. Sims could also continue to welcome visitors to the city with the train depot right behind their building. The intersection of Main Street and the Boulevard continued to grow when the First State Bank of New Port Richey built another beautiful brick building, kitty-corner from the land office. The building was well constructed and included an impenetrable steel safe. Helping to instill confidence, Dr. Elroy Avery took the position as the bank's Chairman of the Board, when the doors opened in 1921. On the southwest corner of the intersection James W. Clark Jr., son of the original settler, built a two-story brick mercantile building. A feed store took up most of the ground floor, and four apartments were located on the second floor. All three buildings are still standing today.

Another prominent building that was constructed during this time was the Palms Theatre. Perhaps a preview of what was to come in the city, the Palms Theatre showed silent movies every Saturday night. Tickets were only fifty cents for adults and twenty-five cents for kids. It became a regular social event in the city for parents to bring their kids to the movies and then visit with their friends on the streets and in the downtown shops and eateries. The Palms Theatre was owned by J.S. Jackson, and although it was rather primitive in its construction, having a dirt floor, it boasted some of the best movie projection equipment available. The Palms together with the Civics Club in Enchantment Park hosted most of the community events, such as weddings, picnics, and holiday parties.

All the new construction that built up New Port Richey's downtown streets were nearly washed away when a devastating category 3 hurricane made landfall in nearby Tarpon Springs. There has not been a larger hurricane to directly hit the Tampa Bay area since that October day in 1921. It brought a storm surge of between ten to twelve feet of gulf waters. The entire Tampa Bay region was affected when torrential rainfall and 100 m.p.h. winds swept ashore. Fortunately, there was no loss of life. The biggest casualty was the citrus groves, namely in Elfers, that lost their harvest. In New Port

Richey, buildings lost their rooftops, many homes were damaged, and some barns and wood sheds collapsed under the deluge.

When the rain and winds finally stopped the entire city was strewn about resembling the appearance of a teenager's unkempt bedroom. One strange phenomenon occurred when the Church of Our Lady, Queen of Peace was lifted off its foundation and turned ninety degrees. The church that once faced south, now faced west. Miraculously, Father Felix, who was actually in the church at the time, was not harmed. When he exited the church and surveyed what had occurred, he simply accepted the will of a greater force.

Well, if that's the way God wants it, we'll just have to leave it that way.

Father Felix

Eventually Father Felix had to rebuild his church, but for the time being, the city of New Port Richey survived a scare. Not even a great hurricane could take the city off its course.

New Port Richey was a developing community heading into the 1920s. With a new highway running through it, a new railroad depot, new utilities of electricity and telephone, new schools and churches, and growing industries of citrus and turpentine, New Port Richey had the makings of a city on the verge of booming. Its citizens had an eye for the future, and most importantly, it had leaders with a vision to get them there. The founding fathers of New Port Richey, Gerben DeVries, George Sims, and Elroy Avery were bound and determined to make their little city the "Gateway to Tropical Florida."

Marjorie Sims on her horse along the Dixie Highway, 1923 brochure.

Home of George and Marjorie Sims next to Enchantment Park

Mule Cart in front of Land Office and Train Depot

Painting of Dr. Avery by Fred Sass

Gerben DeVries with the catch of the day

4

The Chasco Fiesta

In 1922, city business leaders, as part of a Board of Trade, charged Gerben DeVries with the task of coming up with a marketing plan to attract people to their newly constructed city. For inspiration, Gerben needed to look no further than to what was occurring each winter in the city of Tampa. In 1904, Tampa was in a similar position as New Port Richey. Wanting to attract people to their blossoming city, business leaders formed a committee to consider ways to market the virtues of Tampa. On that committee was a former citizen of New Orleans, where for two hundred years the city streets were packed each year with revelers celebrating Mardi Gras. Plans for their own celebration were put into place with the concoction of a mythical story of Jose Gaspar and his attack on the city of Tampa. The Gasparilla Festival was born. Tampa's business leaders dressed in flamboyant pirate costumes and symbolically swash-buckled in the streets under the name of Ye Mystic Krewe of Gasparilla. The festival was an enormous success bringing tens of thousands of people to Tampa. Each year, the boat flotilla, which began in 1911, landed on the downtown banks of Plant Field and the Tampa Hotel. The event officially opened the Florida State Fair, which was held on the grounds since 1904.

Gerben DeVries decided that New Port Richey needed its own story to build a festival around. Instead of pirates, DeVries created a fictional tale around the Indians and Spaniards who fought a battle on the banks of the Pithlachascotee River long ago. He published his story with the title "Chasco, Queen of the Calusas." All money earned from the book and the festival would go to building the new library. To build interest, the New Port Richey Press released parts of the story each week for six consecutive weeks leading up to the festival. The Festival was called the Chasco Fiesta in honor of the heroine of the story Queen Chasco. On January 22nd, 1922 the first excerpt of "Chasco, Queen of the Calusas" was released.

While fishing upon the banks of the Pithlachascotee River, (now called the Cotee River), near the old Indian stone steps at the first palm grove on the west side above Enchantment Park, New Port Richey, on New Year's Day, 1922, Postmaster Gerben M. DeVries made an important discovery... At the base of a palm tree which had been disturbed by a recent storm, he noticed a peculiarly shaped object... The cylinder contained parchments that were badly deteriorated but whole. They were covered with writing in old Castilian Spanish. Enough of it was translated to show that it contained valuable information relating to the early history of the Pithlachascotee River.

New Port Richey Press

According to DeVries, the story contained in the old clay cylinder described a Spanish expedition that arrived from St. Augustine intent on destroying a Calusa Tribe on the west coast. Instead, in a surprise attack, the Calusa captured the Spaniards who were sacrificed in sunset rituals on top of a mound at the mouth of the Pithlachascotee. The only members of the expedition that were spared were a priest, Padre Luis, and two teenagers, Don Phillip and Dona Isabelle. The three of them were made into honorary members of the tribe. Each took on new names; Padre Louis was known as La-ka-no-kee, which meant bearer of the cross, Don Phillip became Pithla, and Dona Isabelle became Chasco. Over time, Pithla and Chasco won over the hearts of the tribe, and Chief Mucoschee accepted the teachings of La-ka-no-kee. The sacrifices ended, and Chief Mucoschee adopted Chasco as his daughter so that she would one day be Queen.

My daughter, in that I have ordered the spilling of blood, thereby thinking to appease the Great Spirit, I am no longer worthy to be king of this my people. With the outgoing tide, I go to join my brother, Hirrigua." Placing a garland of flowers and leaves on her head he further said, "Unto thee my daughter Chasco, I give authority to have dominion over the entire people…. If the people abide always in thy teachings, they will increase in numbers so they cannot be counted; they will never be in want and the days will follow each other with ever new and delightful pleasures.

New Port Richey Press

With the fictitious story of Queen Chasco complete, Gerben DeVries and the people of New Port Richey had the means to build their festival. Never mind the fact that the Calusa Indians actually lived far south of New Port Richey, and they certainly did not practice human sacrifices. But why ruin a good story with facts? The fine citizens of New Port Richey loved the story and bought into it hook, line and sinker. With each installment of the story appearing in the newspaper, momentum began to build for the three-day celebration.

One popular event of the Chasco Fiesta was an election to name the first royal court. Ballot boxes were located at the Central Market and Bavers Dry Goods Store. Each vote cost a penny, and you could vote as often as you wanted. To no one's surprise, Marjorie Sims won the contest for the title of Queen Chasco by 6,000 votes. Barnum Davis was named Prince Pithla, having won by 2,500 votes. The votes were tabulated, and the coronation was made at the Palms Theatre. It was a thrill of a lifetime for a young lady to be named Queen Chasco in front of her friends, family, and fellow townspeople.

I was tickled to death to be voted in as Queen. Somebody in town made our costumes. I wore different necklaces, a white top and skirt, and a wreath of flowers on my head. It was wonderful! The coronation, the boat parade, it was all thrilling!

Lucy Decubellis, Queen Chasco 1948

The first Chasco Fiesta opened on Thursday, March 2nd, 1922 with a parade along the Boulevard. Cars, trucks, and animals were decorated for the occasion. There were carnival games in Enchantment Park along with horse races and car races around the racetrack encircling Orange Lake. At five o'clock was the featured event. A boat parade down the Cotee River was a wonderful sight, drawing crowds of revelers along the banks. At the tail end of the parade was the boat carrying Queen Chasco to an Indian village set up in the park. Townspeople dressed in Indian garb were seen throughout the grounds. Notables included Chief Mucoschee, Padre Louis (La-ka-no-kee), Prince Pithla, and of course Queen Chasco. The ensemble put on re-enactments of Gerben DeVries' now famous story. Enchantment Park was bursting at its seams, full of revelers dressed in festive garb and having a splendid time.

When we were kids we'd go down to the Chasco Fiesta with hats that were woven out of palmetto fronds. If you didn't have a hat on you could be arrested, symbolically of course.

Dewey Mitchell, King Pithla, 1995

The Chasco Fiesta was a grand success not only for attracting thousands of people to New Port Richey, but also in raising more than a thousand dollars for the Avery Library. Two shows, a moonlight cabaret, and a Vaudeville comedy, played to packed houses at the Palms Theatre and brought in nearly four hundred dollars. There were dances, equestrian stunt shows, high wire walking, trapeze performances, and a grand motor boat race down the Cotee River for the Commodore's Cup. The Gerben DeVries concocted Chasco Fiesta successfully brought attention to the city of New Port Richey, introducing many to a city striving to make a name for itself. The Chasco Fiesta continues today as one of the oldest city-sponsored celebrations in the state of Florida.

Chasco Fiesta parade, 1922

Chasco Fiesta boat parade around 1960.

Queen Chasco and King Pithla

Girls dressed in ceremonial costumes

Growing Pains

By 1924 the two Port Richeys had grown apart. Port Richey was still a sleepy community satisfied in going about its business without any ambitions to change. Largely a farming and fishing community, the people of Port Richey were self-sustainable with little need or desire for the city. It was a simple life, and they preferred it that way. New Port Richey, on the other hand, had a more diverse population with their eye on the future. They were well organized and wanted to grow. Driven by the Port Richey Land Company their plans were to make their little city into a destination for affluent northerners.

For the most part, the people who were attracted to Port Richey and New Port Richey came from two different areas of the country. Port Richey tended to attract farmers from Georgia and South Carolina, while New Port Richey appealed to wealthy northerners especially from states like New York, Michigan, Ohio and Massachusetts. There were a couple notable exceptions to this trend. New Port Richey also attracted a group of African-Americans from Georgia. They came to the city by train in large numbers hoping to find jobs in serving the needs of the wealthy population assembling in New Port Richey. The group that consisted of about twenty families lived just outside of town in an area known as Pine Hill, as well as in an area just north of town on the Dixie Highway. They had their own church and school and contributed greatly to the growing work force needed to maintain the town's development. The men largely worked in constructing roads and the women worked primarily as maids in the homes of the wealthy. Another unique group which settled in New

Port Richey came from Finland. Attracted by the warm climate and opportunity for land, the Finns made their homes in a number of Florida towns. One prominent Finn who arrived in 1912 was Emil Nyman who was responsible for New Port Richey's first water system.

Up to this point in time, New Port Richey had relied on the generous donations of time and money by its citizens. The business community and civic clubs worked tirelessly in support of a better community through the organization of charity events and fundraising drives. Through these means, they were able to build bridges, roads, sidewalks, parks, schools, and a library. Enterprising people in business capitalized on the city's growth and speculated on its continuation. Their efforts lead to the addition of key communication and transportation services for the city, namely the electric company, telephone company, and the railroad. With the city population around seven hundred and fifty in 1924, no longer could a few ambitious citizens continue to build and serve the community. The needs of the community were growing with each new house that was built.

As further proof that New Port Richey had indeed arrived, acclaimed orator William Jennings Bryan made the town a campaign stop in his run for President and the Democratic Party nomination. In an interesting connection, the nation's top attorney Clarence Darrow also visited New Port Richey. The two men had faced each other in perhaps one of the most famous cases in history. The Scopes Monkey Trial pitted evolution versus creationism on the national stage.

It was time to put in place the formal government structures necessary for managing the city's future. Government officials needed to be elected to make and enforce city ordinances and to coordinate the garnering and allocating of city resources. On October 27th, 1924, residents voted 201-4 to incorporate the town of New Port Richey. Dr. Elroy Avery was elected as the town's first mayor and sworn into office two days later. Also elected to the city government were a town clerk, marshal, and seven councilmen. Port Richey, on the other hand, wanted nothing to do with being incorporated. The following year, Port Richey became worried that their more aggressive sister city might just gobble them up. In order to keep New Port Richey from annexing them, the town of Port Richey saw no other choice than to become incorporated themselves. By way of City Charter, Charles Hoffman was appointed as the Mayor. The next year, Victor Clark, son of pioneer settler James Clark, took over as the first elected Mayor of Port Richey.

In its first order of business, the New Port Richey City Council adopted an ordinance to accept a gift of land from George Sims and the Port Richey Company. The land encompassed the entirety of Enchantment Park including the Cotee River Community Club, boat launch, boat house, gazebo, a croquet field, and a tennis court. The Park was also the location of a wooden bridge that spanned the Cotee River. Citizens built the bridge by raising funds through a five-dollar pledge drive. In honor of Mr. Sims' generous donation, Enchantment Park was rededicated as Sims Park. The City continued to improve the park when it built a bandstand in 1925.

On January 16th, 1920, the Eighteenth Amendment brought in prohibition. All alcohol production, transport, and sale was illegal in the United States. The mass consumption of alcohol by men in America had had debilitating effects on the workplace and home life. The women's movement combined with the temperance movement, energized the nation to put an end to the negative effects of alcoholism in American society. The economy and families were suffering, and prohibition was the treatment. The problem was that not everyone wanted to follow the prescribed plan. It was the Roaring Twenties, and people wanted to have a good time.

New Port Richey was no different than any city in America. There were bootleggers and smugglers. In the case of Florida, a lot of the alcohol came from Cuba. There was already a great deal of trade going on between the Tampa Bay area and Cuba. Vicente Martinez Ybor imported Cuban tobacco to roll cigars in his Tampa factories. Area cattle ranchers sold their beef to Cuban meat packing companies. It was only natural for Cuban rum and whiskey to find its way to American shores. Sloops from Cuba anchored in the Gulf near the mouth of the Cotee River. Locals in small boats rowed out under the cover of darkness to purchase the booze. To hide it from local deputies, the whiskey jugs were submerged in the bayou and out of site.

Another source of illegal alcohol came from the stills of moonshiners hidden in the woods surrounding New Port Richey. Rival gangs were formed when competition for the bootleg business grew. Deputies regularly patrolled the woods for stills, sometimes resulting in gun battles between gangs and deputies. The area often attracted suspect outlaws. Local legend tells of one famous case. A criminal named on the F.B.I. most wanted list was running from the law and sought refuge down in Florida. Two F.B.I. agents went missing trying to track him down in the woods between New Port Richey and Brooksville. Finally, a U.S. Marshal posing as a butterfly catcher was able to get close enough to the criminal's campsite to apprehend him. The notorious criminal was sentenced to hang.

New Port Richey was a blend of old and new at the time of incorporation. An orderly society depends on its members to follow the law of the land so as not to encroach upon their fellow citizens' right to happiness. Before the city was incorporated and before any ordinances were made, people's lives sometimes infringed on one another's. One example was livestock. Fence laws were not in place in Florida, leading to hogs and cattle routinely roaming the downtown streets.

Our very first shopping trip on Main Street introduced the pig menace… As we were about to enter the grocery store, we were met by a razorback sow, with a cabbage head held firmly in her mouth. Beside and around her were a half dozen of her offspring squealing and grunting. Behind them in hot pursuit was the grocer, with a broom in hand and a torrent of unkindly words pouring out his mouth.

Ralph Bellwood

This was hardly the look you want to attract future land buyers. A fence was put up around Orange Lake, to keep the gators and livestock from straying into the road as they went back and forth to the lake. The fencing also served nicely as a barrier for the racetrack that was used from time to time around the roughly quarter-mile circle road.

New Port Richey became a city right at the peak of the Florida land boom in 1924. People were streaming into the state to escape the winter blues of the north. Over two million tourists each year came down to enjoy the Florida sun. Five professional baseball teams made the Tampa Bay area their spring training homes, bringing a great deal of publicity and visitors to the area. The Chicago Cubs, St. Louis Browns, Philadelphia Phillies, Boston Braves, and New York Yankees all had stadiums in either Tampa or St. Petersburg. Florida land was cheap and made for a very fashionable investment.

Real Estate was big money in Florida and with big money often came corruption. One such case was recalled by J.H. Moran of Boston who purchased land from an agent sight unseen. The agent told him that the roads were as good as those in Boston. However, upon arriving in New Port Richey, Mr. Moran found a different situation.

So, soon after, on a bright May morning in Port Richey, we left the Sass Hotel via auto to view the new El Dorado. After riding seemingly two miles over palmetto roots, stumps, and fallen trees, (but no road) we arrived... I'm going back to Boston and put that agent in jail...But I didn't do so, and as far as I know, that agent is still at large, and I am still a resident of New Port Richey.

J.H. Moran, citizen

By the mid-1920s, many states were enacting Blue Sky laws to protect their citizens from real estate agents selling unseen Florida swamp land. Ohio had a law which forbade certain firms from selling Florida real estate in their state. Some states had laws which prohibited the selling of Florida real estate unless the buyers actually saw the land. Florida was getting a bad reputation right at the peak of the land boom. Even with this growing risk, investors who heard of the great deals were still buying. They were just more cautious about who they did business with and where they invested in Florida. New Port Richey had built a strong reputation, to the point that former U.S. Treasury

Secretary William McAdoo and Comptroller John Skelton Williams visited the city looking to invest their own money. Their appearance helped to enhance the city's credibility during a time of uncertainty.

Another issue that was affecting Florida was that the infrastructure couldn't keep up with the rate at which housing increased. New Port Richey was able to get a leg up on the concerns of its infrastructure when it incorporated and then appropriated money towards better roads, sidewalks, and bridges. They started by paving the roads downtown including Main, Grand, Missouri, Montana, and Delaware. Two years later, with help from the county, Main Street was extended across the river. A new $30,000 concrete bridge replaced the old wooden bridge that crossed the river at Sims Park. Despite the troubles of most Florida cities, New Port Richey felt it was positioned well to take the next step in its growth.

Gathering at Enchantment Park, January19, 1915.

Livestock fencing around Orange Lake.

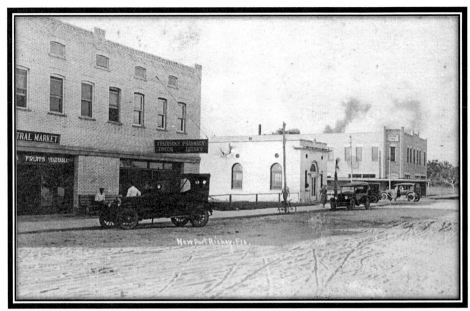

Main Street with Werner Building, Land Office, and Clark Building.

Gulf Utilities Company, New Port Richey

Broadway Connections

In New Port Richey there were great expectations. The Florida land boom was happening at a frantic pace, and people were streaming into Florida in record numbers. In 1925, two and a half million tourists visited Florida. That summer, fifty parcels of land in New Port Richey were taken off the market in anticipation of the increase in demand, then put back onto the market at several times their original price. The improvements continued to be made in the city. A Municipal Water Works was added complete with an extensive sewer system. Most city streets were paved, many with sidewalks and streetlights. All of the conveniences that New Port Richey had were unique in Florida for a town of its size. It quickly became a very attractive destination for the northern elite.

Many of the city's newcomers were people of wealth. James Becker was an industrialist from Ohio whose family owned the Elmore Manufacturing Company which started by making bicycles, but later switched to automobiles. One of the first auto manufacturers in the nation, the Elmore Manufacturing Company invented and developed the two-cylinder engine. Detroit auto manufacturer General Motors felt that the two-cylinder engine was the wave of the future and bought the Elmore Manufacturing Company. With his company sold, Becker started looking for new opportunities. He decided to join Warren Burns, a former executive at General Motors, as a business partner down in New Port Richey. Burns had earlier established the town's electric company and played a large role in New Port Richey's growth and incorporation. Burns, like many of the town's businessmen, saw the potential for real estate development, especially along the beautiful Cotee River.

In 1926, the Burns-Becker Realty Company was established. Soon after, the two northern industrialists, now Florida real estate developers, began breaking ground on a housing development along the Cotee River. Warren Burns had already started a residential development the year before. Old Grove was up river from downtown, about a half mile near Madison Street. The development featured modest homes, mostly off the river, designed for the average family. The Burns-Becker Corporation began work on a more affluent development, Jasmin Point, which ran along the west side of the river and had over a half mile of riverfront home sites. Both Burns and Becker built their mansions in Jasmin Point in 1926. Their homes featured a Mediterranean style architecture with red clay tile roofs, stucco walls and numerous arches above windows and doors. Built about a hundred yards apart, the homes had beautiful views of the river and had private boat docks.

Two past employees of the Port Richey Company also ventured out on their own in the real estate business. Gerben DeVries and Frank Grey sold real estate and insurance, and also rented property for the winter. There were plenty of developments besides those of Burns-Becker. Rio Vista Park and River Heights were developments along the Cotee River and just south of Main Street with lots priced at $3,500. New Port Richey Estates was just north of Jasmin Point, also on the Cotee River. Other exclusive developments were not on the Cotee River but on the waterways of the Gulf of Mexico. Just a couple of miles west of downtown were the island estates of Manor Beach and Bay Shore. Earl Benham, an actor and costume designer whose ties to the movie industry enabled him to sell home sites in New Port Richey as a winter retreat, owned many of these lots.

With courtship of the wealthy continuing, there was a movement towards upgrading the amenities that were desired by the rich. The Palms Theatre was hugely popular in New Port Richey. Although small, it was the only auditorium in the area for hosting events and showing movies. Many people of all ages would go once or twice a week to see the shows, even if its dirt floor and bench seating were far from ideal for attracting potential wealthy buyers into the community. With this in mind, the Richey Amusement Company was formed to build a new elaborate theater that would be a source of pride for the city. The corporation was composed of local investors, Walter Jahn, James Clark Jr., A.E. Leeston-Smith, Charles Barnett, Frank Grey, and Walter Dingus.

The theater was built on land purchased from Leeston-Smith, who was also constructing a mercantile building on the boulevard next to the theater that included a five and dime store. The Richey Amusement Company put forth $50,000 towards the building of the new theater on the Boulevard, just a block off Main Street. The theater was about of 5,000 square feet in size and featured 500 plush seats including 130 in the second story mezzanine. The architecture was similar to the Mediterranean style seen in many of the homes along the river. The exotic Spanish design was very popular in Florida with its tile roofs and arching entries.

The theater began by showing silent movies with the switch to "talkies" expected in the upcoming years. Many romantics were still very supportive of the silent films and couldn't imagine their demise. The theater did include a curtain and small stage for popular vaudeville shows. There was also a pit in front of the stage for a pianist to accompany the films or live shows. It cost 50c for an adult ticket and 25c for kids to see a show.

The speculation in the theater business by the Richey Amusement Company was not without reason. George Sims had been spending his summers in the Long Island hamlet of Great Neck, New York. Located just twenty miles outside of Manhattan, Great Neck was the popular summer home to affluent socialites and the Manhattan theatrical crowds. Longtime resident F. Scott Fitzgerald used Great Neck as his inspiration for his best-selling novel, *The Great Gatsby*. Business leaders of New Port Richey decided to form a recruiting contingent to attract the summer Great Neck residents to New Port Richey for the winter. As members of the Fresh Meadows Golf Club in Great Neck, George Sims, Earl Benham, Warren Burns, and James

Becker were among the committee who sold the virtues of their Florida home.

The plan was to turn New Port Richey into a movie colony, almost a Great Neck South. People connected to the Broadway theater and movie industry tended to stick together in their private lives. By living in exclusive communities of insiders, they were afforded the comfort of living a somewhat private life where they were not continually bothered by the general public. Also, living in close proximity to each other made for the easy organization of swank parties which were the bread and butter of those in high society. George Sims recognized the need for this northern movie colony to have a southern home and had been laying the groundwork for years. In the eyes of George Sims, there was no reason why New Port Richey couldn't be that Florida home they were desired. On January 1st, 1926, the stunning news was announced.

FAMOUS MILLIONAIRES OF
BROADWAY BUY IN NEW PORT RICHEY

Celebrities famous the world over, owners of names as familiar to Paris theatre-goers and Australian music-lovers as they are to the inhabitants of old Manhattan Isle, have bought land in New Port Richey, and plan to build winter homes in this famous resort town, the New Port Richey Press has learned. Recent purchases of building lots in this city, when generally known, will thrust New Port Richey in the public eye as no other community of like size in the limits of Florida can possibly be subjected to the calcium glare of publicity.

New Port Richey Press

The initial wave of celebrities included movie stars, producers, and musicians. Hollywood leading man Thomas Meighan was one of the most famous actors in America. His brother, James Meighan, was a real estate agent who saw great promise in New Port Richey and assisted Thomas in purchasing his property. The Meighan brothers thought they were getting in on the ground floor of something special. Thomas bought a beautiful home site next door to James Becker on the Cotee River. Thomas Meighan was very excited about building a home in New Port Richey and became the main catalyst for other celebrities purchasing land. Most all of the celebrities associated with Thomas Meighan bought land from his realtor brother James. Actress Frances Ring, Meighan's wife, brought her sister, singer/actress Blanche Ring and her husband, comedian Charles Winninger. Leading comedic actress Charlotte Greenwood, who was once married to Frances and Blanche's brother Cyril Ring, bought a lot on Dixie Boulevard overlooking the river with plans to build a sizeable house on it. Actor George Holland can be counted in that group connected to Meighan, as well as famous comedian and actor Leon Errol who was one of the first celebrities to buy property in New Port Richey.

Thomas Meighan wasn't the only famous celebrity attracting celebrities to New Port Richey. Earl Benham, an actor, songwriter and custom tailer to other entertainers, purchased a great deal of land along the Gulf of Mexico bayous and developed the land into the Bay Shore Estates. Benham convinced a thriving young songwriter named Irving Berlin to put a deposit down on a lot in Bay Shore Estates. Berlin had just married millionaire heiress Ellin MacKay, and the couple was being hounded by the press. New Port Richey would serve the perfect getaway retreat for them. Keeping with the musical theme of the development, orchestra leader Paul Whiteman also put money down on a lot in Bay Shore Estates, as did famous singer/dancer Joseph Santley. One notable actor that Benham recruited and who spent a great deal of time at New Port Richey hotels was Raymond Hitchcock. Hitchcock had a young wife, actress Flora Zabelle, who was a rising star first in the theater and then in the silent movie business. The couple were often seen around town running errands and eating at the local restaurants. Often joining them was their young son, who attended the local school during the family's stay in New Port Richey.

Two weeks later, the country's number one movie producer Sam Harris came to town, as did comedian/actor Ernest Truex as a guest of George Sims. Truex purchased a home site in Bay Shore

Estates from F. I Grey Realty Company. Earl Benham and George Sims had been talking about New Port Richey so much up at Great Neck that he and his wife had to come see for themselves.

I expected to find a wonderful place, and you can tell your readers that in my humble opinion I have found it. With the Hitchcocks, the Hollands, the Sims, the Benhams, the Meighans, and the rest of the bunch it looks like good old Great Neck has been half transplanted to this neck of the woods. Well these folks know what they're doing. I've made up my mind. New Port Richey just suits me now and oh, boy, what this town ought to be in just a couple of years.

Sam Harris, producer

The folks in New Port Richey could hardly believe what was happening to their little city still under a population of five thousand. The New Port Richey Press actually printed a photo of Irving Berlin's down payment check, and a wire from Paul Whiteman, confirming to the "doubting Thomases" that this was really happening. In the following weeks more celebrities purchased home sites in Bay Shore Estates. Author/actor/producer Edgar Selwyn, rotund comedian Arthur Deagon, and actor Wellington Cross all purchased property.

Soon New Port Richey was on the map as a popular destination. It wasn't only the theater group that was coming to town, it was anyone who ran in the same circles of the rich and famous. Often people that were traveling to the greater Tampa Bay area saw reason to check out what was going on in the little community just to the north. Two of the most accomplished sports writers in America took a boat ride down the beautiful Cotee River to do a little fishing. Ring Lardner, who was friends with Thomas Meighan, came with his wife and brought with them Grantland Rice, one of the best sports writers in the nation. Also seen on the Cotee River fishing were New York City's sheriff, fire commissioner, and the fire department's chief surgeon.

Meanwhile Warren Burns was busy sticking millions into the development of Jasmin Point which was to include a spacious yacht club on the shores of the Cotee. His own mansion next to Becker's was under construction as well as plans being drawn up for Meighan's mansion two doors down. The Tampa Morning Tribune, with connections to the writers visiting the town, took notice of what was happening in New Port Richey.

Every Florida city has at least one slogan, and it looks as if New Port Richey might call itself **the most famous small town in the world***. Or it might claim to have the largest amount of fame per capita. In fact, pretty soon it will reach the point where an ordinary citizen of New Port Richey will be pointed out by visitors as bearing the distinction of not being famous.*

Tampa Morning Tribune

When Thomas Meighan arrived to close the deal on his home, he brought more news that a syndicate was being formed of movie stars who were going to invest and possibly build homes in New Port Richey. On that list of syndicate members was the name of Gloria Swanson. The world famous actress had starred with Thomas Meighan in the movie *Male and Female*, directed by Cecil B. DeMille. They remained good friends and were entertaining the idea of being neighbors in Florida. Ms. Swanson had been in the Tampa Bay area before when she visited the Tampa Hotel at the age of nine, on her way to Key West where she lived with her family on a military base. Others in the syndicate include Charlie Chaplin's attorney Nathan Burke and film director Victor Heerman.

Homes of James Becker and Warren Burns on the Cotee River.

Filming along the Cotee River 1932

Movie stars Raymond Hitchcock and Flora Zabelle.

Flora Zabelle and Raymond Hitchcock *(courtesy Library of Congress).*

Thomas Meighan and George Sims

7

Leading Man

With so many wealthy people taking notice of the city, it became obvious that New Port Richey was in need of a luxury hotel to serve the needs of its famous visitors. In 1926, the old Sass Hotel, renamed the Enchantment Inn, was still the largest of five hotels in town. Nevertheless, if New Port Richey was going to compete with other Florida cities for celebrity business, they would need a showpiece hotel to give their city the distinction of being an upscale resort town. City officials decided now was the time for action, and went about planning for a first class hotel. James Meighan, the brother of Thomas Meighan and a realtor with a great deal of land holdings in the area, got the project off to a fast start by generously donating nine lots to the city. The land was in a prime location bordering the Cotee River, Main Street, and Sims Park. Meighan donated the land to the city for the specific purpose of building a grand hotel. The only conditions of the gift was that the hotel must be elegant in stature, have at least sixty rooms, and ground must be broken for construction within six months of the date.

In the spring of 1926, the hotel committee seized the opportunity and immediately began raising funds for a $250,000 hotel, of which $100,000 cash was needed to use toward financing the proposition. Shares of common stock were sold at $100 per share, entitling the stockholder to full voting privileges. The community enterprise was incorporated under Community Hotel Inc. of New Port Richey. After only four days $64,000 was raised. After a couple of months, investments had slowed, but the total of $77,000 was good enough to begin the first phase of construction. The initial plans consisted of fifty rooms, a ballroom, lounge, and dining room all of the finest design. The hotel would use steam heat with construction beginning immediately with completion scheduled for February.

Bullied by the news of the grand hotel along with the impressive list of expected clientele, the city was booming at breakneck speed. The progress being made all around New Port Richey was nothing short of astounding. In May of 1926, the newly built Pasco Building on the Boulevard had its open house. Businesses that operated out of the beautiful building with its easily identifiable cupola on top included Roscoe's Drug Store, a bakery, the McMullen Hardware Company and the Western Union Telegraph Company. The Pasco Building brought the count of brand new downtown buildings that started construction in the last year to a remarkable seven buildings. Other new buildings included the Theater, the Leeston-Smith building, the Morey-Bowman Building, and the Maxwell building. All these building were built along Grand Boulevard, which was quickly rivaling Main Street in terms of its grandeur. Two buildings built on Main Street were the Swafford building and the new Pierce Grammar School. Each one of them of the highest architectural quality and adding to the immense charm of the city. Architect Thomas Reed Martin, who is famous for his Spanish and Italian styles, was chosen to design both the new Theater as well as the new hotel. Martin was the same architect used by Burns and Becker for their Jasmin Point mansions. Continuing the Mediterranean style, Martin designed the new Pasco Building as well. By having a continuity in architectural style, the entire town had the look of an exotic and beautiful Spanish oasis.

On the way to future success, the city did experience a setback from its successful beginnings. The Enchantment Inn, formerly the Sass Hotel, caught fire and burned to the ground in May of that year.

The first building of ambitious pretensions erected in the city... reduced to ruins in less than ninety minutes.

New Port Richey Press

Fortunately, the building was relatively empty of guests who tended to return to the north as May rolled around. Mr. Monahan, manager of the Inn, and his wife along with employee Edna Saucier were able to escape the blaze unharmed. Only one guest, R.L. Shope, needed to jump from a second story window into the arms of policeman Charles Cooper. Thanks to a thirty-man bucket brigade, the neighboring Sally Shoppe and Maxwell Buildings were unharmed. The burning down of the Enchantment Inn together with the construction of the new Community Hotel less than one hundred yards away, marked a passing of time for the citizens of New Port Richey from the city's past to its future.

The city of New Port Richey continued to attract attention from celebrities. When plots were sold by auction at River Gulf Point just down river from Jasmin Point, well-known movie star Richard Barthelmess was one of the first to buy. Word continued to spread through all corners of the state of Florida and beyond. Over thirteen hundred newspapers around the country picked up the Associated Press news report that Thomas Meighan had organized a syndicate of New York stage stars to form a movie colony in New Port Richey, Florida. National exposure was the last piece of the puzzle to make New Port Richey a boom-town. To celebrate the city's success, George Sims decided to invite the Governor for a visit.

HON. AND MRS. JOHN W. MARTIN
TALLAHASSEE, FLORIDA

DEAR GOVERNOR: - IT GIVES ME GREAT PLEASURE TO SEND YOU THE FIRST TELEGRAM EVER SENT OUT OF NEW PORT RICHEY WHICH IS BEING DISPATCHED FROM OUR NEW WESTERN UNION OFFICE OPENED HERE TODAY AND WITH IT I SEND YOU AN INVITATION TO PAY US A VISIT IN APRIL...

MR. AND MRS. GEORGE SIMS

Adding to the intrigue and culture of New Port Richey, two museums were opened. The Hub gallery, located in the Swafford Building on Main Street featured the paintings of Fred Sass. Fred and his wife Ollie were the original owners of the Sass Hotel, then sold the hotel to George Sims and others, who renamed it the Enchantment Inn. Fred Sass was widely recognized as one of the top artists in Florida. He honed his artistic skills living in Paris and working under the tutelage of internationally famous artists, Jules Lefebre, Ferdinand Cormon, and Benjamin Constant. His paintings on exhibit in New Port Richey included scenes of the old west, the Grand Canyon, moss covered trees, scenes from around New Port Richey, and even a painting of Mayor Elroy Avery.

Resident A.K. LaMotte had a more bizarre museum; he was a collector of rare art from the Igorot tribe of the Philippines. The Igorot were infamous for their head hunting and head shrinking traditions. LaMotte's collection was one of the most complete in the world. It featured weapons such as head axes, knives, arrows, swords, and blow guns with poison darts. Some of the items were made with gold, silver, and copper fittings. LaMotte also displayed a wooden helmet, hemp jacket, and a head squeezing outfit. Some of the items were more common; wooden boxes, woven baskets, and a wrought iron tea pot. But the main attraction for both the locals and the northern elites was the actual shrunken head. The Igoroti had removed the skull from their enemies' head and inserted hot round stones in its place, allowing the head to shrink to the size of a grapefruit.

There was no doubt; New Port Richey was a town that had everyone talking. So much so, the New Port Richey Press began running a subtitle under its name, "A Famous Old Paper in a Famous New City." The celebrity influence on the city became commonplace. Famous movie star couple Raymond Hitchcock and Flora Zabelle had a son that was close in age to local boy Jimmy Grey.

The Hitchcocks used to send a driver and their son to Jimmy's house each morning to take them to school. At first Jimmy, who would dress up real nice for school, was excited about riding in a limo to school each day. But the novelty eventually became the norm, and he thought nothing of it.

Chuck Grey, grandson of Jimmy Grey

On June 23rd, 1926, the white street lights of New Port Richey were turned on for the first time. Main Street, Circle Drive, and the Dixie Highway (Boulevard) were all lit up in a dazzling display. The following week came the grand opening of the new theater. The theater was given a new title of the "Thomas Meighan Theatre," for his role in attracting some of the brightest stars to New Port Richey and for choosing the city as his home. The theater showed the movie *The New Klondike*, starring Thomas Meighan to an enthusiastic capacity crowd. With the opening taking place in June while the celebrities were out of town, telegraphs of congratulations were received from celebrities like Thomas Meighan and famous comedian Ed Wynn, a frequent visitor to the city, and read to the crowd by Senator Jesse Mitchell. Manager J.S. Jackson, who used to manage the Palms, announced that the new playhouse would have a complete cooling system installed to make the theater one of the finest in Florida. The following year, New Port Richey passed a referendum to allow the Meighan and Palms Theatres to be open on Sundays.

Although Thomas Meighan wasn't able to be at the opening of the theater that bore his name, he was quick to lend his celebrity status to other town functions. He helped out with the dedication of the new concrete Main Street Bridge crossing the Cotee River. The bridge would be very useful to Meighan with his new house being built on the other side of the river. More than five hundred local citizens showed up to see their new local hero dedicate the bridge.

Friends and fellow citizens – I can say this, because I've just signed a contract for the building of my new home at Jasmin Point and workers will start breaking the ground Monday morning. It gives me great pleasure and I am very happy to dedicate this beautiful new bridge. Friends, I wish to state that I decided to locate my residence here after having seen the entire state of Florida as well as other states, and I found this to be the most beautiful and homelike city in the entire state.

Thomas Meighan

Dr. Elroy Avery, then lead the town in a cheer: "Three cheers and a tiger for Thomas Meighan!" The event was followed with pictures taken with Mr. Meighan by the bridge. Many of the pictures taken included the town's children posing with the famous leading man. Finally, Thomas Meighan was the first to drive his car across the Cotee River to the side where his new home was soon to be built.

Thomas Meighan returned to town again two months later to oversee the construction of his mansion on the Cotee River. Using the same famed architect that was used for the building of his namesake theater and the new hotel, Thomas Meighan was very eager for his home to be finished. Years later, Reginald Sims, son of George and Marjorie Sims, recalled the story of Meighan's monitoring of his home's construction.

The Meighans became so absorbed in the construction of their new home that Tom was weeks overdue in Hollywood where he was under contract to make a series of western movies. The producer of MGM telephoned Meighan daily and flooding him with telegrams urging him to report to Hollywood but to no avail. Then one day he appeared in New Port Richey – he had traveled by train from California, then taxied here from Tarpon Springs. But Meighan said he wouldn't leave until his home was finished. Finally, in desperation the producer asked Meighan how much the home was costing him. Anyway, the producer told

Meighan that if he would return to Hollywood with him, MGM would pick up the tab for the home. Meighan got the home as a bonus and it didn't cost him a cent.

Reginald Sims

The Meighan mansion sat on over four acres and 600 feet of riverfront. The acre surrounding the home was beautifully landscaped and the other three acres consisted of citrus trees. The estate included a huge swimming pool (60' x 33') that took 65,000 gallons of water to fill. The house was comprised of thirteen rooms and eight bathrooms including a servant's quarters, which housed two chauffeurs/ bodyguards who drove Thomas and his wife Frances in a huge seven-passenger car. Also living at the residence were the groundskeeper and house keeper who managed the estate for the Meighans year round. Frank Luikart took care of the grounds and his wife Virgie took care of the house. The Luikart family were some of the original settlers of New Port Richey. Virgie's father, Simon Noffsinger, purchased ten acres of land near Green Key for fifty cents an acre back in 1913. Frank and Virgie made $4.75 a week and lived in the mansion for nearly twenty years. Frank raised bees on the property and recalled that the swimming pool was often opened up to the city's children. Meighan's fondness for children was well known, since he often supported children's charities and orphanages. Thomas and Frances enjoyed children even though they never had any of their own.

I was just a little kid...Thomas Meighan would come to town with his chauffeur and load up with kids and take 'em to swim in his pool.

Melvin Draft

More than any other celebrity who came to New Port Richey, Thomas Meighan saw the city as a treasure that was destined to become a winter destination for America's social elite. He readily joined in the crusade to attract people to the city. There was rarely a time when he was not hosting some movie or theater star at his home and selling them on the merits of the city.

I bought here because of the natural beauty and the future I could see for the place. I love this city, I have registered here, I shall vote here and make New Port Richey my home.

Thomas Meighan

Meighan tried unsuccessfully to get a movie he starred in *We're All Gamblers* to be filmed in New Port Richey. The movie was shot in Miami which was further along in its establishment as a motion picture colony. However, Rex Beach, a writer who visited New Port Richey, used the city for his inspiration in his book *The Mating Call.* The book was made into a movie and starred Thomas Meighan, with music by his wife Frances Ring. Produced by Howard Hughes the movie was a big success. Howard Hughes had recently bought Paramount Pictures and signed Thomas Meighan to a five-year contract. Meighan's film, *The Racket*, earned him an Academy award nomination for best picture, and gave his adopted home town a great deal of pride.

Meighan's unabashed affection for the city, among other reasons, continued to attract the country's aristocracy to the shores of the Cotee River. New York perfume mogul William H. Loveland built a colossal mansion near that of James Becker. Robert Montgomery, Boston financier and owner of the Westchester Independent newspaper, bought land to open a subdivision and built a home. In 1928, Dr. Elmer Burnette from Tarpon Springs along with popular novelist, Irving Bacheller, formed an investment group to build an arcade building on Main Street for $60,000.

Making New Port Richey into a movie colony might have been the brainchild of George Sims, but Thomas Meighan quickly became the flag bearer. He had a love of real estate and an obsession with the future prospect of New Port Richey. Some worried when his passion for the city too often took his focus away from his career of making movies. Thomas tried to balance those two interests, but his heart was in New Port Richey. Meighan had a generous soul and a kind heart. He once bailed Rudolph Valentino out of jail. Valentino was only a casual friend of Meighan's, but Thomas bailed him out with no questions asked and no expectation of repayment of the debt. Thomas Meighan had a sterling reputation and a lot of friends in the motion picture business. Those connections greatly benefited the city which mirrored Meighan's image in the public perception of being a friendly place on the rise. With Thomas Meighan's help, New Port Richey was well on its way to being the "Hollywood of the East."

Thomas Meighan helping to dedicate the new bridge extending Main Street over the Pithlachascotee River, October 6th, 1927.

Thomas Meighan Theatre 1926.

Meighan mansion on the Cotee River.

*The setting for "Mating Call" was inspired after
Rex Beach's visit to New Port Richey.*

69

The Hacienda Hotel

Groundbreaking for the New Port Richey Community Hotel happened on August 11th, 1926. It was financed through efforts of the local Civitan Club and built under the direction of the Burns and Becker Company. As is often the case when financing falls short of expectations, the first phase plans become the final plans. Scaled down from the original version, the Mediterranean style hotel was built with fifty rooms, which was ten less than James Meighan's original condition of sixty rooms. The finances of the $100,000 construction expenditure and $30,000 furniture expenditure worked out to $85,000 of stock sold to investing citizens and the remaining $45,000 picked up by a group led by Warren Burns. The Board of Directors were hoping for a New Year's opening, in time for the majority of the winter season.

The hotel featured four main areas for guests to congregate and relax. On the south side of the building there was an outdoor courtyard open to Main Street and surrounded by the hotel on the other three sides. On the North side was another outdoor area. A large terrace spanned from one side of the hotel to the other. The terrace overlooked Sims Park and was shaded by the towering cabbage palms that swayed in the Florida breeze. Whimsical Spanish archways welcomed guests into the building from both the terrace and the patio.

Inside, the main floor salon was filled with elegant furniture, where women could lounge and enjoy their tea and where gentlemen could catch up on the stock market and business news while enjoying a freshly rolled cigar from nearby Ybor City. Next to the salon was the

71

dining room with a long mahogany bar and tables with white table cloths. For special occasions, there was also a private dining room off the main dining room that had nice views of the deck and park. Each winter, there was an around-the-clock staff of cooks, bartenders, bellhops, maids, and butlers.

The hotel had several small bedrooms located behind the kitchen. There were rumors that the rooms were used by harlots when entertaining male guests of the hotel. More likely is that the hired help used the small bedrooms. Since the hotel was open from November 15th to April 15th, seasonal employees needed a place to live while working at the Hacienda. The small rooms may have also been used by any of the valets, cooks, or drivers, which the wealthy guests brought with them on their vacations. Access to the kitchen, a private workroom, as well as a private stairway going up to the second floor rooms, allowed the servants to provide room service, and tend to their duties, unseen by the paying guests of the hotel.

You will find a new sense of luxury, relaxation, and comfort in the big lobby with its massive open fireplace, with its large doorways opening on the terrace on one side and the cloister on the other. Hacienda Hotel service is planned to anticipate, unobtrusively, your every need for comfort and entertainment whether you come to rest or to enjoy outdoor sports and recreations.

Hacienda Hotel brochure, 1926

The fifty guest rooms were each equipped with their own private bathroom, steam heat, telephone, and wall-to-wall carpeting. The rooms were not as large as most luxury hotels, since the goal was for the Hacienda to have as many rooms as possible. Instead, it was possible to purchase a larger suite situated on the corners of the hotel, or to combine rooms through an adjoining door. Rates were manageable at $5 for a single room, or $9 for a double room. The hotel encouraged long-term rentals by offering weekly and seasonal rates, operating much like an upscale resort destination.

Another feature was a hidden tunnel that ran underground from the hotel to the river. However its purpose was not to smuggle booze as many locals speculated. The hotel and most of New Port Richey was only eight feet above sea level. This unique circumstance made it convenient for the removal of sewage. The small tunnel carried the refuse from the hotel to the river. Since the Cotee River was a tidal river, the tunnel was literally flushed out on a daily basis. In fact, most of the homes near the river operated under this same concept. As one local resident noted, "You were far better off waiting until after high tide to go swimming."

About midway through construction the Board decided to roll out the new name for their exquisite hotel. The hotel was christened as the "Hacienda Hotel" on Saturday, November 13th, in a grand ceremony. The Spanish name was thought fitting for the Mediterranean structure which featured clay tiles on the roof, pink stucco walls, and romantic archways. Even halfway through construction, every witness to the ceremony could see that this was a building that would define the city for generations to come. The Hacienda would join the other grand pink stucco hotels in the Tampa Bay area like the Vinoy Hotel built in St. Petersburg the previous year, and the Fenway Hotel of Dunedin, which was constructed at the same time as the Hacienda.

For the name christening, Warren Burns, the master of ceremonies, opened the proceedings, followed by a few short words from George Sims. Yet the keynote speaker of the day was one of the most popular comedians in the country, Ed Wynn. No stranger to New Port Richey, Ed Wynn had been coming to the city for years. He first was introduced to New Port Richey by George Sims who socialized in the same circles as Wynn in the Great Neck theater colony each summer. Invited to visit New Port Richey, Ed Wynn stayed at the Sims house for three weeks. He was looking for a little relaxation, after coming off a successful run of his Broadway theater show, Ed Wynn's Carnival, which ran for 116 weeks. Reginald Sims recalls when Ed Wynn visited his home next to the park.

My father suggested he take his boat and go fishing, but Ed said he couldn't bait or take the fish off a hook. So dad sent a guide, Frank Baschard, out fishing with Wynn. The first day Ed caught several trout – from then on he and Frank went out fishing every day. Then one day, right out of the clear blue, Ed told Dad he had to leave for New York to produce his play. My father asked him how in the world he could start production when he hadn't even written the play. "But, I have written it" Ed replied. It turned out that Wynn had written the entire script sitting in the boat, while waiting for the fish to bite. The play, A Perfect Fool, was a smash hit. It ran for 256 performances on Broadway, before he took it on a nation-wide tour. It became what he was known for, often signing his name with the tag line "A Perfect Fool."

Reginald Sims

A great number of people showed up at the foyer of the Hacienda. Ed Wynn did not disappoint in entertaining the crowd. Like many of the celebrities he was very impressed with the city. He purchased a lot from Earl Benham on the Cotee River with the idea to one day build a home. In between jokes Ed Wynn told the crowd that he thought New Port Richey was "the most beautiful city imaginable." He complimented the citizens for their forward thinking in building such a magnificent hotel. Then encouraged everyone to continue working together and one day "the city will be one of the finest in Florida that will attract some of the greatest people in the north." The people of New Port Richey felt like they had a building that would be the finest of its kind, and now they had their feelings confirmed by an American comic legend.

The Hacienda was undergoing its final touches as the new year began. There were several events leading up to the formal opening including a women's tea party, and a fireman's ball. On Saturday, February 5th, the hotel opened its doors for a public inspection. Excitement was at a fever pitch with over eight hundred curious townspeople showing up to take a close look at what they had been observing from a distance over the last six months.

That the hotel was the subject of unanimously favorable comment, is putting it mildly. That its opening was greeted with no less than acclaim, is nearer the truth.

New Port Richey Press

The formal opening arrived on February 17th, 1927. The Civitan Club, who originally fostered the idea for the community hotel and began the drive for funding, had the honor of hosting the grand opening banquet and dance. Although the splendid hotel was built with the idea of hosting northern socialites on vacation, there was no doubt on this night that this was first and foremost the city of New Port Richey's community hotel. There were two rules put into place for the banquet, by the officers of the Civitan Club. The dress code would be informal and club members could invite as many guests as they wished. One hundred and twenty reservations were taken for the banquet portion of the evening.

The entertainment was of the finest available. Legendary jazz musician Blue Steele and his Orchestra kept toes tapping throughout the night. But this night was dedicated to speeches thanking all those who made the dream of the hotel possible. Club President Charles Hoffman served as toaster of the evening and made the first speech thanking four people for their contributions. Mr. and Mrs. Fred Sass for being "pioneers of our early days," George Simpson, who at 96 years old bought the first stock certificate and was a local political leader, and Warren Burns for serving as the President of the Hotel Company through the building process.

The next speaker was Mayor Edgar Wright, who saw the building of the hotel as just the beginning. "This night marks the date when the barrier is dropped and the starter gives us the word, Go!" He gave great credit to the major financiers of the project including James Meighan who donated the $50,000 plot of land for the hotel. Mayor Wright also introduced Arthur Boardman, who after an extensive search, was named the first manager of the Hacienda. The final speaker of the night was Charles DeWoody, a noted after-dinner speaker, who was a favorite of the local crowd. He chose to cap off the night by giving credit to the man who made the dream of a majestic hotel come true.

The hotel's coloring, the furnishing and every detail were chosen by this artistic gentleman, and when funds were needed, he saw that they were forthcoming. He is indeed the father of the Hacienda, and one of the most beloved citizens in our fair city. Fellow members of the City Club, ladies, and gentlemen, that estimable citizen is Jim Becker.

Charles DeWoody

The opening was a great success, with the only negative being that it came near the end of the tourist season and not at the beginning. Nevertheless, New Port Richey enjoyed the continued influx of the rich and famous. World renowned bandleader Bohumir Kryl brought his touring opera singing stars including famous American tenor Ricardo Martin and popular contralto Frances Ingram. In March, silent movie star Dorothy Dalton, also known as Mrs. Arthur Hammerstein, son of Oscar Hammerstein, checked in at the Hacienda with her friend Mrs. Sam Harris whose famous husband had already purchased land in the city. Famed naturalist Charles Torrey Simpson brought more attention to New Port Richey when after visiting the area remarked in his book, "The Pithlachascotee is a genuine river, and the most beautiful waterway in Florida."

The Hacienda Hotel was near capacity during the winter months and about half that during the hot and humid summer months. Because of this the normal room price of four dollars per night was cut in half for guests during the summer. The rooms were small and adjoined with bathrooms and doors in between, allowing for a guest to purchase a one, two, or three room suite. Many of the wealthy guests would take the three room suites or the larger two room suites that were in the prime corner locations of the hotel.

Local legend tells of the famous movie star, Gloria Swanson, staying in the corner suite which had access to a tower where she enjoyed looking out over the river and feeling the gentle sea breezes. There were even reports that parts of the Hacienda were built with her in mind. For instance, the main staircase had two small arches instead of one large one, apparently so that the archway did not dwarf the diminutive Swanson. The New Port Richey Press announced in bold headlines that Gloria Swanson was expected to arrive in town. This announcement, originating from Thomas Meighan, set the star struck citizens of New Port Richey abuzz. Records of her visit are convoluted, even suspect. Yet the lore of sightings of the starlet and her lover, Joseph Kennedy, have remained over the years, giving both the city and the Hacienda a little extra panache.

Some celebrities who visited the Hacienda or stayed in homes around New Port Richey during this time were actresses Lupe Velez, Madeline Cameron, Ivy Sawyer, and Edyth Chapman. Actors that were guests at the Hacienda that first year included Joseph Santly, George Fawcett, Oscar Shaw, Jack Hazzard, Charles Winnegar, and James Neill. Such star power greatly enhanced the Hacienda and New Port Richey. The vibe in the town quickly went from a remote Florida cracker town to an extravagant resort destination. Jesse Lasky, the founder of Paramount Pictures, stayed at the Hacienda with his family.

One day I'll join Thomas Meighan and others in a colossal motion picture studio enterprise in this vicinity.
Jesse Lasky, Paramount Pictures

The entire city felt the effects of the Hacienda's popularity and responded to the push for continued improvements and fueling the budding economy. Besides doing well in fostering the movie star business, New Port Richey was also attracting retail business. Several national chain stores began operation on the Boulevard in the newly built Leeston-Smith building. The Pool-Hoffman Drug Store converted to national brand, Rexall Drugs, opening the store next to the Meighan Theatre. The change allowed customers to have access to the entire line of Rexall pharmaceuticals without leaving town. Next to the Rexall Drugs was Bailey's 5c, 10c, and 25c Store followed by the Atlantic and Pacific Tea Company Store, better known as the A & P

Grocery Store. The stores all opened to promising reviews and brought a modern downtown market center to the New Port Richey. Seemingly overnight, the line of products made available to the citizens got dramatically better with the opening of these three national chain stores. Both the Leeston-Smith building and the Pasco building across the street, with George Sims as its most prominent owner, had no trouble renting their entire buildings out within a couple weeks of their openings.

One additional business of note was started on the Boulevard just down the street from the Leeston-Smith shops. Stanley Robinson was a former All-American quarterback at Colgate University who went on to a successful coaching career at Mississippi State and Mercer College. The famous coach had been released by Mercer and decided to get into the auto repair business while waiting for his next coaching opportunity. Stanley Robinson's Seminole Garage was opened in a brand new $50,000 facility on the Boulevard in 1926. The garage was one of the largest and best equipped in the area.

After ten years, the old Tug and Grunt Railroad was bought out by the Seaboard Airline Railroad in 1927. They continued service to New Port Richey with whistle stops in the morning and in the evening. Most of the materials that were coming in were coal for the electric plant, and building supplies for all the new construction happening in the city. Lumber, turpentine, and citrus were produced in the area and sent out to market. But mostly the train was used by passengers. Locals would leave in the morning and travel to Tarpon Springs or Clearwater, then catch the evening train back home. On trips to Tampa, a transfer had to be made in Tarpon Springs, stretching the trip to as long as a two-and-a-half-hour commute. Often people traveling to Tampa would stay the night and come back the next day. And of course the train was used by northern travelers coming down for their winter vacation.

*Romanticized painting of the Hacienda by renowned
New York artist Alfred S. Landis.*

The Hacienda main entrance on Riverside Place.

Hacienda lobby and dining room.

Patio of the Hacienda facing Sims Park.

The Squire

With the opening of the Hacienda, New Port Richey had the signature hotel, which would help make their city into a premier winter resort destination. There was plenty for guests to do while they vacationed in the city. Most activities centered around the river and gulf for swimming, fishing, and boating. There were also the resort mainstays of tennis, horseshoes, card games, badminton, and dancing to live music. Evening entertainment was available at both the Meighan Theatre and the Palms Theatre. However, there was one thing that people of wealth were accustomed to, that was not yet available in the city: a prestigious golf course. There was one golf course near town developed by N.E. Bowden, but it was more of a municipal course than a ritzy resort golf club. A couple other golf courses were of similar quality, without appeal to the upper class. To remedy this need, Warren Burns and Jim Becker went about building a magnificent golf course adjacent to their property of Jasmin Point that stretched down the west side of the river.

The golf course was scheduled to be built on 180 acres of land that was situated between the Cotee River and the Gulf of Mexico. The location was thought to be ideal for its dramatic views of the water on most of the course. Burns and Becker obtained title to the land for nearly $200,000. Their plans were to build one of the most beautiful golf courses in the entire southern United States, which would attract home buyers to the area and specifically to their Jasmin Point development. Much of the land was purchased from A.K. LaMotte, whose home near the river was included in the purchase with the intention of transforming the home into the golf course clubhouse. The tract of land had frontage along both the river and the Gulf of Mexico. It also featured bayous and lakes to make it a very attractive setting for an illustrious golf course. There were also plans to convert a small lake located by the clubhouse into a swimming pool. The first nine holes (but not the clubhouse) would be built in the first stage using a $300,000 allotment, and open for the winter season.

The project was similar to Soundview Golf Club in Glen Cove, NY, which was built with membership fees used towards the construction of the course, with additional funds accrued through the sale of villas surrounding the course. A committee was created with some of the biggest names in town. Meighan, Benham, Sims, Burns, and Becker served to guide the development of the course and obtain memberships. By purchasing a membership to the golf club for five hundred dollars, members were also given part ownership of the course. Burns and Becker had great confidence in the course being highly successful, similar to the courses in what they saw as a comparative community of Boca Raton on the east side of Florida.

In order to make the golf course an attractive destination to wealthy golfing enthusiasts, the committee knew they needed a well-known golfer to be associated with the course. There was no question who they wanted for the job. As long time members of the Fresh Meadows Country Club in Great Neck, New York, Thomas Meighan, George Sims, and others went about recruiting the club professional of Fresh Meadows to be the club professional of their new Jasmin Point Golf Club. This was no ordinary golf professional however, this was the one of the top golfers in the entire world.

Standing all of 5' 5" tall, Gene Sarazen, born Eugenio Saraceni, shocked the golfing world in 1922, when he became the youngest player to ever win the U.S. Open. At the age of twenty, Sarazen not only won the U.S. Open, but proved it wasn't a fluke by winning the P.G.A. Championship that very same year. Tremendously popular, the charismatic Sarazen was on top of the golfing world. His exciting matches with rivals Bobby Jones and Walter Hagen served to help spread golf's popularity in America during the 1920s. Five years removed from his stunning debut on the world stage, Gene Sarazen was crafting his game at the Fresh Meadows Golf Course just outside Flushing, New York, when he was approached by the men from a little town on the Cotee River in Florida.

Gene Sarazen was convinced to make a trip to Florida and survey the land. The committee asked Sarazen to make recommendations as he saw fit for the layout of the future golf course. Their hope was that in the process Sarazen could be convinced to serve as the club professional and manager. After his second trip to New Port Richey, it was clear that his role in the golf course and in the city had been advanced. At a luncheon, where the highly touted golfer was introduced to members of the community, he didn't mince words.

New Port Richey is the place to live, and I say this after seeing all of Florida. New Port Richey will be a more attractive place to live when it has a fine golf course such as the folks here are planning. You can have the most beautiful course in the state over there across the river. I intend, some day, to make New Port Richey my winter home.

Gene Sarazen

On that very same visit a parcel of land sandwiched between the river and the course was chosen for the building site of Sarazen's new home. The home would be located across the street from Thomas Meighan, who he had become good friends with while up in Great Neck. Although not as extravagant in size as the nearby homes of Meighan, Burns, Becker, and Loveland, the house would be designed by the same Sarasota architect that had designed all the grand buildings of the city, so the Sarazen home would undoubtedly carry the same state of distinction in its style. One unique feature of the golfer's home was a tremendous trophy room to display all the awards he had acquired and those he was sure to claim in the future. As to the construction of the golf course, Sarazen had a few ideas.

In building your course, I told Mr. Burns this morning, you want to build a course which will be attractive to everybody, a course which the duffers can play and get as much enjoyment out of it as the pro. A series of roughs beautified with wild flowers, and paths from the cup to the next tee lined with hibiscus and other native flowers should be an asset. A golfer likes to play in beautiful surroundings. You have a chance here to build a little gem of a course, and the grasping of the chance is up to you.

Gene Sarazen

The townspeople immediately embraced their new fellow citizen as they had done earlier with the arrival of Thomas Meighan, who by now was referred to as "Our Tom" by citizens. Gene Sarazen, like Meighan, was about as pleasant of a man as you could know. He and his lovely wife Mary made friends quickly in town. Ralph Bellwood, a New Port Richey resident who arrived to the city about the same time as Gene Sarazen, remembered how he was very comfortable in New Port Richey.

We enjoyed many conversations with the wiry Gene, who was the epitome of good taste in dress, as he walked about the street in knickers and a sweater.

Ralph Bellwood

One benefit of having Gene Sarazen living in the city and managing the Jasmin Point Golf Club was that he represented New Port Richey at all his tournaments, which amounted to a lot of free advertising for the city. When Sarazen teed off from the first hole of every tournament, the announcer would always introduce him as, "From New Port Richey, Florida, Gene Sarazen." During his first winter in New Port Richey, Gene drove to Miami Beach where he won two tournaments. The local paper welcomed Sarazen home with the following article:

We congratulate our plucky fellow citizen. His double victory personifies the spirit of New Port Richey. It is a similar spirit of friendliness that welcomes the newcomer from the time he arrived in New Port Richey's famous hotel, the Hacienda, until he decided to make this his permanent home.

New Port Richey Press

Sarazen continued the routine of using the courses of Great Neck for his summer home, and then living and golfing in New Port Richey during the winter. The local boys got a kick out of serving as caddies at the Jasmin Point Golf Club. Some even caddied for Sarazen himself. The Luikart boys, Francis and Clarence, served as caddies, as did Jimmy Grey. Jimmy, who owns the distinction of being the first boy born in the city, recalled the excitement during those early years.

New Port Richey was in its hey-day. Something was always going on. Glittering fashionable balls at the Hacienda, or dances at the big boat house at the river's edge, partying at homes, three golf courses, and then there was the Meighan Theatre.

Jimmy Grey

Sarazen liked to golf at the other courses in the area as well as Jasmin Point. He set course records at both the Tarpon Springs and Dunedin golf courses. Gene and Mary were also very involved in the Our Lady Queen of Peace Catholic Church. Father Felix had started the church years ago when there were only seven families attending. Since that time the patronage had grown and Sarazen noticed that the priest could use some help getting around town. So Sarazen bought Father Felix a brand new car. Father Felix, not wanting to accept such a nice gift meant only for him, asked Sarazen if he minded if the car could be sold and the money from the sale used for buying new pews for the church and helping the congregation as a whole. Gene and Mary Sarazen were more than happy to help.

Horseback riding was a popular pastime around town. Marjorie Sims was often seen on her horse galloping around town, on the trails and dirt roads which were plentiful. In the winter of 1928, Gene

Sarazen used horseback riding as one of his physical regimens to get into shape for the coming golf season. That spring he enjoyed more success than he had in years previous. When a reporter from the Associated Press asked Sarazen what he attributed to his return to winning form, Sarazen responded with a nod to his hometown.

A horse down in New Port Richey, Florida. I feel right this year for the first time since I have been playing serious competitive golf. There are several reasons, but I place the horse first. All winter I rode horseback all the time I wasn't playing golf, eating or sleeping. I have never been really well. My health has been bad off and I knew that if I did not get myself in shape, I wouldn't win any more championships. Of course I can't take the horse out on the golf course with me and, as that is where I am spending my time now, I will forego my riding exercises until next winter. But that old horse will be waiting for me.

Gene Sarazen

The golf course at Jasmin Point did not turn out as nice as everyone had hoped. Warren Burns was not quite as confident when it came time to actually putting up the front money required to start the project. The course was scaled back with only nine holes being constructed in the first phase. Under this new plan, the course did not reach to the bayou and Gulf waters, which were key components in making it the scenic course it was projected to be. Instead it featured only a single water hazard over a small pond. Without any elevation changes or fairways bordered by water hazards, the course was rather mundane. Few northerners were drawn to the area with only a nine hole course, not even on the water. Although there were some northern golfers who were attracted by the Sarazen name to play Jasmin Point, the course was dependent on a steady flow of local members. With the average citizen of New Port Richey more comfortable with a fishing pole in their hands than a golf club, Jasmin Point struggled to make ends meet.

As for Sarazen, he enjoyed four years as a resident of New Port Richey. Probably the most interesting aspect of his time in the city was his invention of the sand-wedge. The one part of Gene Sarazen's golf game that was giving him trouble during the 1920s was his inability to effectively get out of the sand traps. He thought that a club specifically designed for the sand would help him in conquering the dreaded traps. So Sarazen tried to find a way for a club to help bring the ball up even while he was swinging down. The idea for the sand-wedge hit him while flying with his friend Howard Hughes.

When Hughes's plane took off, the flaps on the wings came down, and my father made a connection to the flaps and the flange of a golf club. By adding more weight to the back, the club would slide through the sand and help the ball pop up.

Mary Ann Sarazen, Gene's daughter

There were other clubs out there that attempted to do the same thing. Most of the clubs were used in Scotland but with mixed results. Sarazen's rival, Walter Hagen, had a large sand wedge with a hickory shaft that was deemed illegal by the PGA. Sarazen went to work on his own idea during his winter stay in New Port Richey. He began tinkering with his prototype at the Scofield Huddleston Garage on the Boulevard next to the high school. The owners of the garage were nice enough to let the local hero use the garage as his laboratory for creating the wedge.

I called the Wilson Company and had them send me twelve niblicks and I went to the hardware store and bought solder and rasps and files, and spent four or five hours each day filing away until I got it just right. The New Port Richey Course wasn't a very good one, but it had an excellent trap, right behind my house. It was there that I tried out my sand-iron, hitting thousands of shots each week, making adjustments back in the machine shop, testing the improvements until I had the sand-iron perfected.

Gene Sarazen

Sarazen's wedge was almost identical to the modern wedge with a steel shaft. The technique of hitting behind the golf ball and exploding it out of the bunker was also a Sarazen concept. Gene used the club to great success winning both the British Open and the U.S. Open that year. Fearing that the club might be taken away from him by event officials, he kept quiet on his invention. He kept the club in his bag with the club head facing down so as not to draw attention. Each night he would smuggle it into his hotel room under his coat. Once he was assured that the club was legal, he shared his invention with the world. When he finally broke his silence the club became an instant hit. Over his career, whenever he saw his sand wedge in other golfer's bags, in tournaments around the world, it always brought a smile to Gene's face.

It probably should have been called the Sarazen wedge.
Arnold Palmer

Gene Sarazen and the local paper boy.

Gene Sarazen is one of only five golfers to win
all four of golf's major championships. (photo courtesy of Sarazen Foundation)

Mary Sarazen and Flora Zabelle play
at Jasmin Point Golf Club.

Sarazen's New Port Richey Municipal Golf Course around Orange Lake.

10

Great Neck South

With Thomas Meighan and Gene Sarazen firmly on board with the creating of a movie colony in New Port Richey, everything seemed to be falling in place for the once pie-in-the-sky idea to actually happen. As long-time and recognized residents of the New York movie/theater colony of Great Neck, who ventured south each winter to their New Port Richey homes, Meighan and Sarazen had considerable sway over other residents of Great Neck to do the same.

These people (at Great Neck) simply followed each other to this Florida town in the winter, making it their part-time headquarters while in the state. In summer-time, New Port Richey mostly returned to being just another hot and dusty southern town.

Glen Dill, Suncoast News

With each winter season, the ritual returned of the famous and wealthy spending their days in the New Port Richey sun. The local contingent continued to welcome them with open arms as they made their way south, following the migratory flights of the birds. The celebrities were given royal treatments by the citizens and by each other, welcoming each other much like you would your friends back to school after a summer apart.

On one such occasion a welcoming party was sent out to welcome home Broadway star Flora Zabelle, wife of movie star Raymond Hitchcock. Several celebrities including Mr. and Mrs. Earl

Benham, Mr. and Mrs. Gene Sarazen and local dignitaries including George Sims loaded up in cars to meet Flora as she crossed the Cotee River Bridge. The caravan of cars numbered more than thirty as they escorted Flora to the downtown area where the city band played a celebration of her triumphant return. At which time the new mayor, James Clark, presented Mrs. Hitchcock with the keys to the city.

With all the folk from Great Neck down in New Port Richey it is no wonder that the editor of the Great Neck News, Hal Lanigan, also came down with his wife for a two-week vacation at the Hacienda. Covering their visit to the city was guest columnist Charles Kahles, creator of the Hairbreadth Harry nationally syndicated comic strip. The highlight of the trip was without a doubt a fishing excursion into the Gulf in which Mr. Lanigan caught a four hundred pound kingfish. Lanigan had the time of his life and proclaimed that the theater crowd of Great Neck, New York, had found another paradise.

We encountered another Great Neck, an appetizing smart little duplicate of our wonder city.

Hal Lanigan

New Port Richey became filled with producers, directors, writers, singers, actors and actresses from Great Neck each winter. It was a private social club that simply moved back and forth across the country. The townspeople could hardly believe what was happening. At any moment they could see a world famous actor or singer walking past them on the streets of their little town. The celebrities of Great Neck were making themselves right at home.

February of 1928 also saw the likes of novelist Charles Maigne and Chicago Pulitzer prize-winning writer George Ade who was one of the first members of the Jasmin Point Golf Club. Famous song writer Walter Donaldson came to town to visit his friend Thomas Meighan. Donaldson wrote some of the biggest hits of the twenties including "Yes Sir, That's My Baby," "Makin' Whoopie," and "My Blue Heaven."

Also that month Florida Governor John Martin stopped in New Port Richey to give a speech while campaigning for a U.S. Senate seat.

Another interesting person who chose New Port Richey as his home was Richard Conover, a former U.S. Open tennis semifinalist. Most citizens never realized that the elderly man playing tennis at the Sims Park tennis court was actually one of our country's best tennis players as a young man. To add to the impressive background of Mr. Conover was the fact that he was the grandson of Richard Stockton, a signer of the Declaration of Independence.

Despite the land boom coming to an end, New Port Richey was still a target of wealthy investors bullish on the city. One of the richest men in the country, multi-millionaire August Hecksher, came for a visit the second week of February. Hecksher owned thousands of acres in Florida including land around New Port Richey. He was in town to inspect a site for an oil rig.

Although this is my first visit to your city, I like it very much. I believe the oil well we expect to start very soon will be the means of making a real city, such as you dream about.

August Hecksher

Fellow multi-millionaire and president of the New York Chamber of Commerce, Irving Bush, was in town the following week and purchased 200 acres near Miller's Bayou and another 1200 acres four miles east of town. Local real estate man George Sims toured both financiers through the city. The land purchases by two of the most highly regarded speculators boded well for New Port Richey. In the rest of Florida, the land boom had come to an end by 1928. City leaders were optimistic that the forecast for New Port Richey's growth could stem the tide.

There were some very practical ways that the growth of the city can be seen. Mrs. Clyde Lapham, operator of the city's telephone system, made an interesting request of the citizens. Up to now the standard procedure had been to ring Mrs. Lapham and ask her to connect them with another person simply by telling her their name. She had a good memory, but the population had grown to nearly a thousand by 1928, and she simply could not remember the telephone number of everyone in the city. From now on, people would have to use their phone directories and tell Mrs. Lapham the number that they would like her to ring up.

Another indicator of growth came in the fall with the opening of the schools. The area had two grammar schools, the Pierce Grammar School on Main Street, and the Elfers Elementary School which absorbed the students from the Seven Springs School when it closed. Gulf High School on the Boulevard across the Cotee River had served as the lone high school in the area. It opened its academic year with their highest enrollment, topping one hundred students for the first time. The school proudly graduated nineteen students that spring with the Gulf High graduates wearing caps and gowns for the first time. The Junior/Senior banquet was held at the Hacienda Hotel. The hotel successfully fulfilled a dual role, that of a grand resort for northern vacationers, and that of a wonderful facility for the locals to host community gatherings.

With the fall of 1929 came the annual preparations for winter visitors from the north. Warren Burns, who had a great deal of money and time invested in New Port Richey's development, became particularly concerned that everyone in the city do their part. As a businessman he saw the land boom coming to an end in Florida and knew that for New Port Richey's economic arrow to continue to point up, the city would have to continue to be the showcase resort town that he and others had worked so hard to create.

Mr. Burns wants property owners to prepare for the influx of prominent visitors this coming season by dressing up their property, and also urges upon the city the beautification of the principle streets and parks.

New Port Richey Press

This was expected to be the biggest winter season ever for New Port Richey. The city was riding a wave of success and they wanted to maintain momentum. George Sims sent a telegram from Great Neck, New York, touting the arrival of a banner season.

Unquestionably every available house in town will be occupied this winter and the hotels will be packed to their capacity. This means building operations will increase.

George Sims

True to his word, all seven hotels in New Port Richey were nearly completely booked for the winter season, including all fifty rooms of the Hacienda. Other improvements made for the fall arrival included the Palms Theatre being renovated and the Meighan Theatre adding sound. In preparation for the season, all the merchants in town had their shelves fully stocked with the latest items. Sims Park added picnic tables, tennis courts, volleyball courts, horseshoe pits, and a new dock on the river. With expectations of larger yachts arriving this winter, the Cotee River underwent dredging to create a deeper channel out to the gulf. Up to this time, the biggest yacht on the Cotee was that of Charles DeWoody.

Another attraction that was added this year was the newly built municipal golf course around Orange Lake. Gene Sarazen felt that the kids needed a place to learn to play the game. Many people were new to the sport of golf and perhaps a bit intimidated by the course at Jasmin Point. In order to have a developmental course where both the young and old could learn the game and have fun, a small course with holes that were only 30 to 80 yards long was created around Orange Lake. It featured 30 sand traps, 18 greens, and one lake in the middle, which was a hazard on every hole. The racetrack had to be taken down to make way for the municipal golf course. Gene Sarazen pitched in with the planning of the course, and the New Port Richey Men's Club took over the maintenance responsibilities. Meanwhile the Jasmin Point Golf Course had plans for an additional nine holes, a casino, a clubhouse, and a pavilion.

Sarazen continued to attract attention to the area. Sports writers routinely made the trip south in the spring to cover spring training games and other athletes during their off season training. It was nice for them to get out of the winter snow and into the Florida sun for their own relaxation as well. One such writer who was one of the most-read columnists in the country was Grantland Rice. The Chicago sports writer spent more than one winter in New Port Richey hunting and fishing.

The Cotee River is a winding little stream, the scenery could not be more entrancing. There is no prettier river trip in the entire country.

Grantland Rice

On one occasion, years later, Grantland came to Florida as part of a Paramount Pictures project in which world class athletes were filmed in their training routines. In this particular project the fitness regiments of two of the most popular sports heroes, Babe Ruth and Gene Sarazen, were compared side by side. The short films were called "Building Winners."

Meighan and Sarazen at Jasmin Point Golf Course.

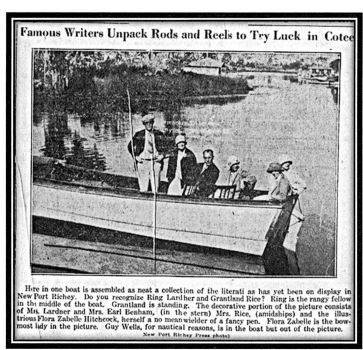

Famous Writers Unpack Rods and Reels to Try Luck in Cotee

Here in one boat is assembled as neat a collection of the literati as has yet been on display in New Port Richey. Do you recognize Ring Lardner and Grantland Rice? Ring is the rangy fellow in the middle of the boat. Grantland is standing. The decorative portion of the picture consists of Mrs. Lardner and Mrs. Earl Benham, (in the stern) Mrs. Rice, (amidships) and the illustrious Flora Zabelle Hitchcock, herself a no mean wielder of a fancy pen. Flora Zabelle is the bow-most lady in the picture. Guy Wells, for nautical reasons, is in the boat but out of the picture.

New Port Richey Press photo)

Grantland Rice fishing with Ring Lardner, Feb. 5th, 1926.

Nicholas Schenck of MGM with the Meighans and Sarazens.

The Palms Theatre, bought by famous comedian
Ed Wynn before it burned down.

11

The Crash

American investors were very optimistic after the conclusion of World War I, and they helped grow Florida's economy with tourism and land speculation. Yet the unrestrained spending of the Roaring Twenties met head on with the harsh reality that the market could no longer sustain the frantic pace of growth. On October 29th, 1929, Wall Street experienced the worst stock market crash in the country's history. Although the markets would slowly recover over the next few months, the effects of the crash would be felt from New York to New Port Richey over the next decade of the Great Depression.

Yet the story of "Black Tuesday" did not even make the headlines of the New Port Richey Press. Instead the talk was of the upcoming winter season and the return to New Port Richey of Meighan, Sarazen, Becker, and the rest. The two new golf courses were declared ready for play. The Orange Lake Municipal Golf Course was very successful in luring both locals and the northern guests who were not comfortable playing on the larger courses. The Jasmin Point Golf Club was officially opened when a famous foursome teed off. The foursome included Thomas Meighan, Gene Sarazen, movie star and comedian Leon Errol, and movie director Henry King. King just directed a movie at Tampa's Rocky Point called "Hell Harbor." It was Thomas Meighan who talked him into the location. With the return of the northern crowd, the Hacienda was set to re-open for the winter season on November 15th. There was excitement over a minstrel show opening at the Meighan Theatre, and motor boat races that were scheduled on the Cotee River.

If anything the economic outlook was looking up in New Port Richey, at least for the moment, unaffected by events on Wall Street. The City Council announced that all its bills were paid and they were delighted to report a $16,500 surplus in the city's coffers, which was a first in the city's brief history. Continuing the good news, power rates from the Gulf Utilities Company dropped from ten cents to seven cents per kilowatt-hour, saving the city even more money. Three local businessmen, Frank Grey, Rollo Draft, and Henry Dingus opened a new business called the Gulf Pine Products Company and hired thirty employees. The principal products were tar and rosin from the surrounding pine trees. Also opening in New Port Richey, the newly constructed Maxwell Building on the Boulevard across from Orange Lake. The building housed a tea room that promised to be an attractive gathering place.

Celebrity interest in the city showed no signs of declining. Hall of Fame baseball player and owner of the Washington Senators Clark Griffith and his wife were guests of the Beckers at their home on the Cotee. Griffith was known as "The Old Fox," and led the league with an ERA of 1.88 in 1898. Hometown hero Gene Sarazen won a stone-crab eating contest hosted by noted Chicago writer George Ade, a frequent visitor to New Port Richey. Sarazen returned to the city after training with Heavyweight Champion Gene Tunney. Sarazen attempted to join Tunney on his training runs at five in the morning, but admitted quitting on his training resolution with the Champ; "I broke after three agonizing days."

As always the Meighans served as hosts to the nation's elite. Frank Case, author and owner of the famous Algonquin Hotel in Manhattan, stayed for a visit. Cartoonist Billy DeBeck, creator of the very popular nationally syndicated Snuffy Smith cartoons, visited the Meighans. One of the most powerful players in the movie industry, Nicholas Schenck, owner of MGM Studios, was a guest at Meighan's home on the Cotee. Schenk and his wife, along with Mrs. Arthur Loew, came to New Port Richey for some rest and relaxation. Arthur Loew, who was the owner of MGM studios, passed away in 1927 leaving control of the movie production company to Nicholas

Schenck. MGM was one of only a few movie studios to survive and in fact flourish during the Great Depression. This left Nicholas Schenk as the eighth richest man in America during the 1930s. Talk around New Port Richey was that MGM was looking at the city as a possible location for filming its movies.

The excitement of the season would turn to concern as the year went on. Unlike Jasmin Point, Bayshore Estates stumbled in its development. The location of Bay Shore Estates in the jungle-like bayou miles from the center of the city, and the absence of Earl Benham as a full time resident of New Port Richey, made it difficult for the development to get off the ground. The economic collapse in the country made matters even worse. Although the development started with great optimism, the poor economy worried many of the buyers who pulled out of their contracts, and the homes were never constructed. Speculation turned as to whether the Jasmin Point development would meet a similar demise.

After the stock market crash, Warren Burns started to put a lot of pressure on the city to continue its growth as a Florida winter destination. His hope was to attract more people with capital who would open businesses and invest in the city as he had done. A lot of effort was made towards the beautification of New Port Richey. There were contests for the best kept homes, with prize money awarded by Thomas Meighan. Citizens joined a cleanup of the Cotee River banks. Warren Burns continued to make his pleas to the city as he has in the past, saying that "future visitors are sure to look with disfavor on any evidence of neglect or lack of care." Citizens of New Port Richey were aware of the nation's economic turbulence and began to wonder if making their city pretty was the best use of their time and money. Warren Burns, now a City Council member, was perceived to be acting out of desperation, which gave citizens a reason to feel apprehensive about the prospects of their city.

That worrisome feeling was on full display when the town showed up to welcome home Gene Sarazen after a big win in the Aqua Caliente Golf Tournament in Mexico in 1930. Sarazen had just been awarded ten thousand dollars, the richest purse ever given to a professional golfer. Mayor Barnett decided to seize the opportunity and give Sarazen a hero's welcome.

I was met at the station by the mayor of New Port Richey and a cheering throng bearing a noble banner, "Welcome Home, Gene." The Mayor, who was also the president of the bank, hugged me and congratulated me and heartily suggested that I deposit my check from Agua Caliente in his bank. I told him I'd think it over. After some reflection, I sent my check for deposit to my New York bank. It was a fortunate thing I did.

Gene Sarazen

By November of that year the natives were even more restless, causing Mayor Barnett to once again preside over a meeting to reassure the citizens that everything was all right. The news of the nation sinking into a depression was beginning to seep into the city, which to this point had not felt its effects. About one hundred concerned taxpayers showed up for the town meeting, worried that the city was going bankrupt.

While our bonded indebtedness does not greatly exceed $500,000, other cities this size are carrying indebtedness of more than a million each.

Charles Barnett

Although the city was able to keep its head above water during the depression, there were a few changes that needed to be made in order to do so. Many city administrators had their salaries cut by one-third. The city's newly installed street lights were turned off except for a few vital areas at the request of the police department. The Avery library at first closed down completely, but thanks to the contributions of Dr. Avery, the library was able to re-open on a twice a week schedule. In another sign of the times, Gulf High School suspended playing football from 1933 until 1938.

Charles Barnett may have been successful in keeping the city from going under, but he wasn't so effective in keeping the bank

102

afloat. Even though he told his stockholders that 1930 was certain to be the bank's "best year ever," the bank fell drastically short of that prediction. On June 13th, 1931, the First State Bank of New Port Richey was forced to close its doors due to the strains of the depression. Nothing puts more of a scare into a town than when their local bank runs out of money.

The Meighan Theatre had plenty of adversity of its own during the years after the market crash. With the rise of *talkies,* the theater invested in the finest sound equipment. Thomas Meighan himself had the honors of pushing the button that started his first talking film *The Argyle Case* at the Meighan Theatre. He was introduced that night by Madeline Cameron, a famous actress in town for a visit. The allure of watching movies with sound brought big crowds to the theater during the spring of 1930. With the slow-down of the summer, the theater went back to showing silent films, using those months to revamp their sound equipment which wasn't operating with the highest quality.

By the fall of that year, the Meighan Theatre had a change in management companies. John Freeman, who previously operated a theater in Daytona Beach, was the new leaseholder of the theater. It reopened in the fall on a limited schedule of Friday through Sunday until demand warranted opening for more days. Even though talkies were again shown, the crowds never returned. In 1934 the Thomas Meighan Theatre succumbed to the pitfalls of the depression and discontinued operations.

Another victim of the stock market crashing and the subsequent depression was the Jasmin Point Golf Club. There is a giant red leather bound book with the words "Jasmin Point Golf Club" emblazoned on the cover, meant to record all the members when they arrived to play the course. The two-inch thick book has only five pages of signatures and hundreds of empty pages of disappointment. With the unfortunate failings of the golf club, Warren Burns either was unable or unwilling to pay the salary of the course professional. Gene Sarazen, one of the best ambassadors for city, was out forty thousand dollars. What happened next was the worst possible scenario for New Port Richey.

Sarazen was understandably angry and he stepped down from his position in 1930 after two years of consulting and managing the course and being "the Florida greeter for my fellow Lambs." Another New York golfer, Al Ciunci, took over for Sarazen at both Jasmin Point and Fresh Meadows. But in 1932, Sarazen sued the golf club and Warren Burns for not fulfilling the agreement of his contract. He stayed in New Port Richey, a place he greatly enjoyed living, through the next season. In 1934 Gene Sarazen sold his house on the Cotee River and ended his relationship with the city. With Sarazen gone, the city decided against fixing up the Orange Lake Municipal Golf Course that Sarazen was instrumental in developing, and instead voted to tear it down. The two courses he designed were both laid to ruin, in a sad ending to what had once been a great story. Gene Sarazen, the man whose name was so closely tied with New Port Richey, was no longer a resident of the city.

To add insult to injury for New Port Richey, Sarazen's fame quickly surged again with one swing of his golf club. The same year Sarazen cut ties with New Port Richey, he made one of the most famous shots in golf history while playing in the Masters at Augusta, Georgia. Trailing Craig Wood by three shots in the Masters Championship, Gene Sarazen was on the 15th fairway some 230 yards from the hole. Taking a four iron, Sarazen hit what became known as "the shot heard around the world" when he drained it for a double eagle. To commemorate the shot, there is a bridge leading to the 15th green at Augusta that bears the name Sarazen Bridge. He would go on to win the Masters, which made him one of only five golfers in history to win all four of the golf's major championships.

With one of the city's finest residents having already packed his bags and moved away, New Port Richey would undergo another tragic loss. The same year Sarazen moved away, Thomas Meighan was diagnosed with cancer. Terribly sick and in need of proper treatment, he retreated back to his home in Great Neck where he underwent a major surgery the following year at Doctor's Hospital in Manhattan. After battling the illness for two years, Thomas Meighan passed away at his home in 1936, at the age of 56.

Thomas's wife, Frances Ring, sold the house in New Port Richey and stopped visiting the city. For eight years the Meighans had been coming to Florida and spending their winters in New Port Richey. Probably more than a hundred famous movie stars, producers, singers, composers, writers, and musicians visited New Port Richey during those eight years. The majority of them came because Thomas Meighan told them it was the most beautiful city in Florida. Meighan was obsessed with making the town into a movie colony. His tremendous influence cannot be overstated. Now that he was gone, the steady migration of famous people from Great Neck to New Port Richey came to an abrupt end.

In one horrible year, New Port Richey lost its two most famous residents and its most influential ambassadors. If that weren't enough, the city also lost a member of its local nobility. Dr. Elroy Avery, the "Grand Old Man of New Port Richey," and its first mayor, died in December of 1935, at the remarkable age of 91. Other men important to the livelihood of the city who lost their lives during that time included Raymond Hitchcock in 1929 and James Becker in 1931. The city of New Port Richey was built on people, not industry. Losing key people in this city was akin to another city losing its main employers. The lifeblood of the city was gone. In the midst of the Great Depression, and with World War II just around the corner, the city that had been thought to be destined for greatness would never recover that illustrious form.

View down the Boulevard.

First State Bank of New Port Richey.

The Goodyear Blimp visits New Port Richey.

Mansions along the Cotee River.

12

Moon Lake Ranch

In June of 1929, before the stock market crashed, an area businessman, Ed Haley, led a group of investors in purchasing more than 8,000 acres of land just east of New Port Richey. The land surrounded Moon Lake, a beautiful 127 acre lake, formed from the Cotee River drainage basin. The lake was 38 feet at its deepest point and surrounded by spectacular cypress trees. Haley had success prior to the bust in capitalizing on the growing tourism industry of the area. He had built a number of successful enterprises including the popular Fort Harrison Hotel in Clearwater. His plan for the Moon Lake property was to build a sportsman's paradise for hunting and fishing. Vacationers staying in the Tampa Bay area had heard the stories of the lakes and rivers teeming with fish and the forests filled with wildlife. Yet for those who had invested in the cost of a trip to Florida, there was a demand for a fully stocked wildlife refuge to guarantee that they wouldn't be going home without a good hunting story.

The project started in 1933 when eight thousand fence posts were installed to hold up an eight-foot-high wire fence that stretched for fifteen miles around the property. Next, the property was stocked with a variety of birds including quail, ducks, geese, African partridges, India and Java peafowl, wild turkeys, pheasants, and wild guineas. Haley also brought down a thousand Virginia and English fallow deer to the preserve. There were multiple lakes on the property. All of them were fully stocked with largemouth bass and other desirable fish for the sportsmen. For the next three years, there was no shooting allowed within the fenced limits of the preserve, allowing the wildlife to take hold and multiply in the newly created environment. There was a rumor that Babe Ruth was able to coerce Ed Haley into permitting him on the property to hunt, while he took a break from his spring training regimen. Besides Ruth, there was one other notable exception to the no hunting rule - it was open season on all alligators. A full time game warden was hired to manage the gator hunts. Other animals that were hunted at this time included panthers, tomcats, hawks, and owls.

We must rid the water and the land of all the natural enemies of the game. Among these are the alligators and the hawks.

Ed Haley

Haley knew that in order for the hunting preserve to be profitable he needed to capture the guests for a long period of time by making a variety of attractions available. For this reason, the Moon Lake Gardens and Dude Ranch was created. The ranch was a great employer for New Port Richey at a time when its citizens needed it most. At the high point nearly two hundred men were employed for the construction of the ranch, and hundreds of men women and teenagers were employed in the service areas. When finished, the majestic ranch included a grand lodge, riding stables, three horse trotting tracks, fishing piers, boardwalks, exotic gardens, a casino, and dining options. Outside one of the restaurants was a fish pool which allowed for guests to catch their dinner using small nets.

Dozens of cozy cabins were scattered about the property. The cabins were furnished with rustic furniture made from nearby cypress and cedar trees. Thirty Kentucky-bred riding horses were waiting in the stables for guests to take them on more than fifteen miles of well-groomed riding trails. The gardens were particularly impressive. Beautifully landscaped, the well-manicured grounds had a wide variety of foliage and flowers seen in every direction. Besides the affluent tourists, who were the target guests of the ranch, the local Tampa Bay population were encouraged to drive to New Port Richey then make the short trek to Moon Lake Gardens for a day trip.

Admission to the grounds was 25 cents for adults and children under twelve were free.

When guests arrived to the Moon Lake Ranch, they checked in at the main lodge which was a sight to behold. Built from the tall long leaf pines that were in abundance on the property, the rustic lodge was impressive.

There were chandeliers made from cypress knees ingeniously put together and wired for hundreds of light bulbs. A majestic stone fireplace with a huge log mantle heated the lobby during the winter months. Hanging on the walls, or perched about on niches, were mounted animals and heads as well as hawks and owls. A large stuffed alligator, so real looking that many a guest shy away from it, lay sprawled on the floor.

Ralph Bellwood

No less dramatic in its appeal was the Great Dance Hall. The largest dance floor in the southern United States was made of polished maple and was 246 feet long and 70 feet wide. Four imposing stone fireplaces were staggered along one side. When the Moon Lake Dude Ranch opened on New Year's Day in 1937, the wildly popular Paul Whiteman's Orchestra reportedly was given the honors to play the Great Hall.

Distinguished quests enjoyed the sprawling ranch including Cornelius Vanderbilt III and other members of the illustrious family. Many of the same celebrities that frequented the Hacienda found themselves driving eight miles east on the winding dirt Moon Lake Road to take in the festivities of the Ranch. People like Charles Winninger, Rex Beach, and Charlotte Greenwood all took in the activities at Moon Lake Gardens. In 1938, Ed Haley was able to convince members of the Florida legislature to hold an informal caucus at Moon Lake Gardens to choose a new Speaker of the House.

Ed Haley was not without controversy. A known bootlegger, Haley brought the finest booze and wine served from a sixty-foot-long bar. The liquor was probably purchased through some less than

111

reputable sources that Haley was known to keep in his company. Due to Haley's infamous reputation to skirt the law, many racketeers and gamblers found their way to Moon Lake. The casino featured slot machines, poker, and dice. There was a rumor that the notorious Chicago mobster Al Capone stayed at the ranch under an assumed name. The likelihood of this is remote. Capone did visit Tarpon Springs in February of 1931, checking out the sponge industry while staying with a friend in St. Petersburg. Moon Lake Gardens had not been started at that point. Upon returning to Chicago Capone went to court after the F.B.I. had busted him on tax evasion. He was sentenced to prison, and served from 1932 to 1939. After his release from Alcatraz, he emerged mentally incapacitated due to complications from late stage syphilis, and spent the remainder of his life in seclusion at his Palm Island home.

Another famous sportsman that was rumored to go hunting at Moon Lake was Babe Ruth. What is known is that the Sultan of Swat liked to visit the area to hunt and fish. He often was seen relaxing at the Os-O-Waw Inn in Aripeka, a town about fifteen miles to the north of New Port Richey. He first started fishing around Aripeka in 1919 when he was with the Boston Red Sox who held their spring training down at Plant Field in Tampa. The Bambino continued to spend time relaxing in the area when he was with the New York Yankees who had their spring training in St. Petersburg from 1925-1934. According to a local folk tale, Ruth supposedly lost one of his World Series rings in the pit of an outhouse at the hotel. Another spot that Ruth, and Yankee second baseman Tony Lazzeri, frequented when in Aripeka, was a little cabin at Littell's Fish Camp.

On December 7th, 1941, things would change dramatically for the United States and for Moon Lake Ranch. The attack on Pearl Harbor brought America into the Second World War. With the war came efforts to ration goods at home, which included tires, cars, gas, and food.

With gas in short supply, the tourist industry in Florida suffered greatly. Long trips by the tin can tourists were no longer feasible, nor was a resort built upon lavish spending. To compound problems, there was an employee shortage at the Moon Lake Ranch. The young men had gone overseas and women were called upon to fill the necessary roles to support the war efforts. In 1941 the Moon Lake Gardens and Dude Ranch closed its doors.

Ed Haley wasn't the only Pinellas County entrepreneur who purchased large tracts of land in western Pasco County during this time. Two other men bought up thousands of acres of land just to the south and east of New Port Richey. Jay B Starkey, a rancher from Largo, purchased 16,000 acres of land in 1937 around the eastern portion of the Anclote River. In 1942, William H. Mitchell, who owned large portions of land in St. Petersburg and the Clearwater Countryside area, purchased 13,000 acres south of the Anclote River in what would later be known as the Trinity area. Mitchell's sons Jack and Jim ran the ranch and drove the cattle north to Hudson down highway 19 before it was paved. W.H. Mitchell also bought the Moon Lake property from Ed Haley after the resort closed. Yet the Mitchells decided to sell the Moon Lake property after sons Jack and Jim were shot at while tending cattle at the remote location.

The earliest known settlers on the property that Starkey bought were the McNeill family, who arrived sometime in 1882 having bought 61 acres under the Florida Internal Improvement Fund. James and his wife Martha were farmers with three children. Their fifteen-year-old daughter died of smallpox and is buried on the property. James McNeill served in the Confederate Army and later was a teacher at Baillie School. Remains of their homestead can still be seen at Starkey Park.

Jay B Starkey first became interested in Pasco land when he saw the free ranging cattle business declining in Pinellas County because of the continued growth and development of the area. The land of Pasco County was relatively unencumbered and ideal for ranching. Together with his business partners, the Cunningham brothers, they found some Pasco County land and started the CS Ranch.

I was somewhat familiar with the area having camped on the Cotee River for several days in 1933, helping two old friends gather their cattle in the area. I was interested in that land, make no mistake about that. It was close to home and good range and timberland... As it turned out, in twelve years the timber would have paid for the land eight times.

Jay B Starkey

Over the years, Jay and Blanch Straub Starkey sold over 8,500 acres to the Southwest Water Management District to protect the land and water source against development. Always the conservationist, Starkey continued to take steps of preserving the natural land for future generations. The Starkey family went on to donate more than four thousand acres for use as the beautiful Jay B Starkey Wilderness Park, located off Starkey Boulevard just east of New Port Richey.

The Seven Springs area along the Anclote River was first settled by Samuel and Elizabeth Stevenson sometime before 1867. The Stevensons had seven children all remaining in the Seven Springs and Elfers area. The Mitchell family ranch, which rested in the Seven Springs area, was bordered by the Starkey Ranch to the east, and the Boyd Ranch to the west and south. The Boyd Ranch was also known as Boot Ranch and was marked by a large boot statue that became a well-recognized landmark over the years. The ranchers in the area were very neighborly towards each other, often helping each other out on cattle drives and large projects.

In downtown New Port Richey, the city was trying their best to make it through the depression. In 1939, a municipal building was built to house the library, City Hall, and the fire station. The town jail was in the back of the fire station where police chief Pop Barga had his office. It was built under the Work Projects Administration, which was a New Deal economic recovery program that provided jobs to the unemployed for the construction of public buildings, roads, and bridges. Under the program, the city had to provide for ten to thirty percent of the costs. To accomplish this the city used portions of the Werner building, a two story white brick building that was previously

114

built on that Main Street location, in the construction of the new Municipal building.

Even though the focus of the city was no longer in trying to make New Port Richey into a movie colony, there was still the occasional celebrity that the city added to its extensive list of famous citizens. In 1941, an eleven-year-old boy moved into a Grand Boulevard bungalow with his family. At the time, he was just a bright young boy who attended two schools in New Port Richey.

I knew kids at both the elementary and high school. This was because I spent a half a day in the sixth grade and a half-day in the seventh. My mother must have convinced the principals I was smart enough to be in the seventh part of the time.

James Irwin

The Irwin family bought their house from Fred Howard, a former Mayor of New Port Richey, who like Aaron Richey years before, moved to Tarpon Springs where he became Mayor of that city. Unfortunately, James' father was unable to find steady work in New Port Richey and was forced to move the family to Orlando after only one year in New Port Richey. The Irwins would have remained forgotten citizens had it not been for an amazing accomplishment by James who would bring him fame the world over. Thirty years after living in New Port Richey, Apollo 15 was launched from Cape Canaveral carrying astronaut James Irwin to the moon. During the 1970s "race to space," astronauts took on celebrity status nationwide. James Irwin is one of only twelve men to ever walk on the surface of the moon. He also garnered fame as the pilot of the first lunar module which allowed the astronauts to explore vast areas of the moon's surface.

James Irwin never forgot his time spent in New Port Richey. Irwin returned to the city years later when local resident Walter Casson Jr. invited the astronaut to the 50th anniversary of the First Baptist Church where James and his family worshipped years before. The Irwin family were drawn into the church while taking a walk around Orange Lake. The moment was fondly remembered by James and he gladly accepted the invitation to return.

Jim flew into Hidden Lake Airport off of Ridge Road. I picked him up in a light blue limo from North Funeral Home. He was so nice... the most regular guy you'd ever seen. We became good friends and he returned to New Port Richey several times.

Walt Casson, Jr.

With a few exceptions, the thirties were a complete contrast to the excitement of the roaring twenties. Times were bleak in New Port Richey during the depression. To keep spirits up, many people followed the local baseball team. Home games were played on the ball field next to the Hacienda between Main Street and Orange Lake. Stockman and Casson were the team's pitchers, throwing to catcher "Peanut" Whitney. Jimmy Grey was at first base, James Caleigh at second, and Al Shendel in the outfield. Their coach was Frank Grey who had a solid reputation for teaching the fundamentals. It was a small park, but every Sunday afternoon the stands were filled with fans rooting on the home team. Times were hard, but hearing the crack of the bat and watching a Jimmy Grey home run sail over the fence allowed the locals to forget their misery.

Baseball in New Port Richey

Great Hall of Moon Lake Ranch.

Jim Irwin on the surface of the moon.

Future astronaut Jim Irwin (left) outside his New Port Richey home.

13

Man in Black

The 1940s were marked by the U.S. involvement in the Second World War. New Port Richey sent over one hundred of its own to help the cause. Back home there were shortages everywhere during the war. One dairy farmer, Izzy DeCubellis, was left as the primary supplier of milk for the town. The boys too young for the war helped at the dairy farm, milking more than one hundred cows and delivering bottles of milk throughout the city. Gasoline rationing meant that tourists were no longer coming to Florida to spend their money. Food and clothes rationing lead to a slowdown of the economy. Everyone was sacrificing to keep the troops well supplied during the war.

The war finally came to an end, after the U.S. dropped two atomic bombs on the cities of Hiroshima and Nagasaki. When President Truman made the announcement that the war was finally over, sirens blew in New Port Richey.

Folks gathered along the main streets and with their neighbors; many wended their way to churches to pray and give thanks to God. About 8:30 an impromptu parade of several score automobiles preceded by the fire department drove over most of the city and Port Richey, blowing horns and calling gladly to friends as the car drivers and occupants passed the homes of this locality from which over 100 fighting men and the women of the armed forces had left to serve their country and all democracy.
New Port Richey Press, Aug 14th, 1945

When it was all over, the combined effects of the depression and the Second World War, put an end to the momentum that the city once mustered. The city was no longer prosperous economically, and it was no longer intent on becoming a winter home for the rich and famous. New Port Richey had returned to being a forgotten, out-of-the-way, sweltering, Florida town. What once was impressive during the 1920s was now disappointing during the 1950s. With very little going for the city, home prices plummeted to among the nation's lowest. Very few people were making any kind of money in New Port Richey, causing the price of goods and services to fall to some of the lowest levels scene in the country.

Yet, as luck would have it, what seemed like a negative, became a positive. New Port Richey became a place that had one of the lowest cost of living indexes in the entire country. The city once the destination for those looking for an extravagant lifestyle, now was the destination for those desiring a frugal lifestyle. The lavish parties of the Roaring Twenties were replaced with simple and quiet relaxation in the 1950s.

In the 1950s, New Port Richey began to advertise itself as a retirement community. Northerners could maintain their primary homes up north and still afford a modest and inexpensive home in Florida. In 1955 you could buy a two-bedroom, one bath wood framed home with a carport for only $3,500, and a two-bedroom masonry home for only $6,000. A far cry from the mansions built on the river ranging from $50,000 - $150,000 during the glory days of the twenties.

The focus of the New Port Richey business district also made a switch. Traffic was diverted from the old Dixie Highway along Grand Boulevard to the new highway being built west of the downtown area. With traffic no longer streaming through downtown, retailers looked to move where they could get more exposure. During the late 1950s and early 1960s, US-19 expanded into a four lane highway that replaced the old Dixie Highway as the main thoroughfare between New Port Richey and St. Petersburg. Scenic parts of the Dixie Highway remained as Alternate Highway 19, while other parts simply reverted back to being a local road, like Grand Boulevard in New Port Richey.

As time went by, downtown buildings struggled to maintain tenants, losing out to the competition of brand new strip malls along Highway 19.

Located between Highway 19 and the Gulf of Mexico, a new housing development called Gulf Harbors was opened in 1960. Howard Burkland from Chicago spent eight million dollars dredging the Gulf, creating canals and boating lanes. A byproduct of all the dredging was that fishing in the area became significantly better since the water was brought further inland and the fish made more accessible. As had become a general practice in Florida, a golf course was built in the middle of the development. Yet, the course was designed with poor irrigation which led to dry fairways and the abundance of pesky sand spurs that would adhere to the golfer's shoes, socks, and pant legs. Despite the problems with the golf course, Gulf Harbors flourished due to the highly affordable home prices. Two and three bedroom homes, many situated on the man-made canals and equipped with boat docks, could be had for between $5,900 and $19,900.

What really opened up Florida for the masses was the advent of air conditioning in homes. During the fifties and sixties, homes with window air conditioning units were the envy of people without them. Once you had one, you wondered how people could have lived in Florida without one. By the 1970s Florida became an even more comfortable place to live when window air conditioners were replaced by central air conditioning. Like the 1920s land boom, Florida underwent another population explosion when northerners could enjoy the comforts of their Florida homes deeper into spring and even year round.

With the quality of life getting better due to the comforts of air conditioning, and the cost of housing being among the cheapest in the nation, Florida's west coast became a retirement paradise. By 1970 the median age in New Port Richey had shot up to sixty-two. Many retirees came to the areas of Florida where they felt most at home. New Port Richey had a high population from the Midwest, so people from those states felt comfortable in joining others with a similar background and heritage for the winter. There were also noticeable population changes to cities that hosted spring training sites for local baseball clubs, for the same reason of familiarity. The Yankees attracted New Yorkers to Tampa, the Phillies attracted Pennsylvanians to Clearwater, and the Blue Jays attracted Canadians to Dunedin.

In 1961, *Consumer Reports* wrote that New Port Richey was the most affordable place to retire in the entire country. The article was spotted by Ezra J. "Pop" Carter and "Mother" Maybelle Carter. The Carters joined the thousands of others headed to the New Port Richey area when they purchased a home on the Cotee River just west of the Hwy 19 Bridge. Maybelle was part of the Carter Family Singers, an American Folk Music institution since the 1920s, best known for their popular hit "Keep on the Sunny Side." Over the years, numerous family members sang and played with the family band. Maybelle's daughter, June Carter, went on to win five Grammy awards. In 1968 June married Johnny Cash and the two of them became country music's most beloved couple. When Maybelle passed away in 1979, she left the bungalow on Sunset Boulevard in Port Richey to June and Johnny.

For more than thirty years Johnny Cash and June Carter Cash were frequent visitors to their home at the mouth of the Cotee River. Johnny loved to fish and get away from it all. Like many residents of the area, he saw the great contrast of the noise of Hwy 19 and the quiet of the Gulf.

The highway is so clogged with traffic most of the time that people talk about it the way Californians talk about earthquakes or New Yorkers talk about crime, and in some of the souvenir shops you can buy T-shirts boasting I Survived U.S. 19. Still, once you're on our little street, on Pop Carter's front porch with the river right across the pavement from you and your boat bobbing at the dock, waiting to zoom you out into the open waters of the Gulf just a few hundred yards away, all that stuff could be in another country. Here you have the tide, the meeting of freshwater with salt, the seabirds and marsh birds and land birds.

Johnny Cash

For the most part the local people gave Johnny and June their space. Town folk were often alerted to Johnny being in town when they saw the giant tour bus parked out along Sunset Boulevard or on Hwy 19. Yet, they rarely ventured down Sunset Boulevard where the Cash family lived in their little bungalow.

The house itself is quiet and comfortable, and it's not at all grand in the manner of Cinnamon Hill or our main home on Old Hickory Lake. It's just a regular Florida family bungalow from the early part of this century — 1912, I believe — wood-framed, with painted clapboard and a big screen porch in front. It reminds me a lot of the farmhouses you see in the hotter, more northerly parts of Australia. Unlike there, though, our neighbors are close. Next door is only twenty feet away. That helps us feel less like celebrities, and the people in the neighborhood help in that regard, too. They're friendly, but they allow us our peace and quiet. Strangers knock on the door sometimes, wanting to say hello or get an autograph, but not often enough to bother us.

Johnny Cash

Terry Armstrong was a neighbor of Johnny and June Cash as a little girl, and described the Port Richey neighborhood along the mouth of the Cotee River as a slice of old Florida.

You could ride your bike down to the fish house and get a soda and a moon pie for a quarter. The bait shop had a wooden floor and had boats tied up to the dock that you could rent.

Terry Armstrong Stanley

The neighborhood also had a historical site right on Sunset Boulevard. What was called the Oelsner Mound was a hill made of dirt, shells and animal bones and used for religious rituals by the Tocobaga Indian Tribe more than a thousand years before. Martha Oelsner, the social matriarch and colorful character of the neighborhood, owned the property it sat on. Known as "Aunt Martha" to neighbors, she had an interesting story of her own. Martha was the adopted daughter of millionaire beer importer and brewer Rudolph Oelsner of upstate New York. When she was very young, Martha had a son by a man that Rudolph did not care for, feeling that he was after the family fortune. The child's name was Rensleo Oelsner (last name spelled backwards). He drowned at the age of six. Then after a court battle in which the husband claimed abuse by Martha, Rudolph allegedly paid the man to go away.

On a train heading to Port Richey, Rudolf Oelsner passed away, leaving just Martha and her mother Dora to start their new life. They filled their Port Richey home with works of art collected from around the world. The art and antiques, including some from King Henry VII, were destroyed by fire in 1961. They rebuilt their house on the same lot and Aunt Martha became an important part of the unique social tapestry of the old Sunset Boulevard neighborhood.

One of Johnny Cash's favorite things to do when he came to town was to visit one of the stilt houses out in the gulf. Johnny became friends with a local man, Des Little, who would often take Johnny out to his stilt house to fish in the Gulf. The first stilt houses, or fish camps as the locals call them, were built around 1915. At their peak there were as many as twenty-four of them off the Pasco County coast. Anyone willing to put in the time and effort to build a home could do so under squatter's rights. Building a home took a lot of hard work.

I went out there and took a rod and where the rock wasn't too hard, I put my pilings down. The first one's real hard. We'd go out Saturday afternoon and work like hell until dark. Dig a hole with a jet pump, put a board in the hole and walk the piling up. That's one of the hardest jobs you'll ever run into in your life. You ever try to take an estimate while you're standing in a boat, bobbing up and down?

Des Little

In 1968 Hurricane Gladys ripped through the gulf decimating the stilt houses. Of the twenty-four, half were completely destroyed while the other twelve were repaired or rebuilt entirely from the pilings up. Since that time, the Florida legislature put an end to any new stilt houses being built. Over the years, those twelve have been allowed to maintain their stilt houses under the protection of being historic buildings. The stilt houses are used a lot like ice houses are used up on the northern lakes. Sure, there's fishing going on, but the main reason people go out to the stilt houses is just to get away for a little while. Out on the water there is nothing but the smell of the salt air and the sound of the waves and seagulls. A good place to leave your worries behind, drink some cold beer and recall some stories with an old friend or two.

On one occasion, the friend that Johnny Cash brought out to Des's fish camp was the Reverend Billy Graham. The famous preacher had ties to the area, having graduated from Florida Bible Institute in Temple Terrace in 1940. The college later moved to the New Port Richey area where it was renamed Trinity College. Johnny and Billy became longtime friends, often meeting in the area. Pete Little, Des's son, remembered that during the last ten years of his life, Johnny was very dedicated to God, the Port Richey area, and to his family. To repay Des for use of his fish camp over the years, Johnny once bought Des a Toyota pick-up truck and left it in his driveway. "Johnny was always big-hearted like that," recalled Pete.

Johnny Cash was grateful for the good will he received from all his Florida friends and neighbors. He was especially appreciative for the area police departments and the work they did keeping people safe. On December 5th and 6th, 1980, Johnny Cash performed two shows at the Gulf High School gymnasium to benefit the New Port Richey and Port Richey Police Departments. Johnny had been coming to the bungalow on the Cotee River since 1962 when he was first courting June Carter. Just before his death in September of 2003, Johnny and June sold their house on the bayou. For forty years Johnny Cash was a loved and respected member of the community.

Johnny Cash's closest friend in New Port Richey during that time, was Des Little, who seemed to be a person who lived a life of good fortune. Not only was he fortunate enough to gain the friendship of a country music icon, he was also one of the first winners of the Florida Lottery. Des's luck continued beyond picking winning lottery numbers, into winning high stakes games. In 1967, Des Little took over ownership of the Hacienda. According to local gossip and one family member, the Hacienda was won in a gambling game when Robert Semple, a partial owner of the Hacienda put his share of the Hacienda's title into the pot. They were playing a game in which people bet on serial numbers of dollar bills they had in their pocket. Des Little won the bet and instantly became majority owner of the Hacienda. Records show that a new hotel manager named Roy Benedict took over managing responsibilities at the Hacienda when Little took ownership. Shortly after, Robert Semple and his wife left New Port Richey on a long vacation.

Johnny Cash and Billy Graham at Des Little's fish camp.

*One of twelve stilt houses in the Gulf of Mexico near
the mouth of the Pithlachascotee River.*

Home of Johnny Cash and June Carter Cash on the Pithlachascotee River.

Johnny Cash toasting Michaeline and Des Little's anniversary. 1978

14

Donnie Brasco

A bad freeze hit the orange groves around New Port Richey in the 1960s, damaging thousands of trees. The desperate farmers sold their land to hungry developers, eager to put up more homes for retired workers of the northern auto and tire industries from Michigan, Ohio, and Illinois. During the late 60s, 70s, and into the 80s, New Port Richey and Port Richey were inundated with hundreds of small two bedroom newly constructed homes. Housing developments such as Regency Park, Embassy Hills, and Beacon Square were selling houses below $10,000.

Yet the unfortunate nature of the retirement real estate business was that elderly homeowners eventually passed away and left their homes to relatives up north. The relatives up north didn't have a use for the home, so they either sold it at a fraction of the value to investors, or they hired a leasing company to rent out the property. In both cases the eventual occupants of the homes usually fell into lower income brackets and often were transient. Homes were no longer well maintained and fell into disrepair. Bankruptcies, foreclosures, vacancies and irresponsible renters became prevalent causing the area to resemble an abandoned wasteland. Other retirees who found themselves no longer living in a quiet retirement community decided to sell their homes and move out of the area, continuing the downward spiral. Even the snowbirds, who were only in Florida from Labor Day to Memorial Day, were forced to leave when their houses were broken into and robbed during their scheduled absence.

Crime and poverty had a firm grip on the once thriving city. There was still the steadfast local population that represented the heart and soul of the city. However, all the attention had drawn away from the quaintness of the traditional downtown and towards the fast-paced activities of Highway 19. The highway served the needs of the downtrodden population with numerous liquor stores, strip clubs, and pawn shops. There was an exceptionally high number of homeless people pushing shopping carts, or riding old bicycles rigged to serve as a makeshift mobile home. Many of these people turned to drugs and alcohol in an attempt to forget their troubles, only to lose their lives to the oncoming traffic speeding along Highway 19.

There was little notice in 1979 when a bottle club opened in an odd octagon building on Highway 19 just south of New Port Richey in Holiday. King's Court, as it was called, was a former tennis club converted into a social club. The club was leased from New Port Richey attorney Richard Milbauer, who coincidentally worked out of the old Port Richey Land Office. Tony Rossi, an undercover F.B.I. agent, leased the club, and ran it as a high stakes gambling club to attract the attention of New York Mafia families who began to expand their business into Florida. The F.B.I. wired the club for sound and video, while surveying the Mafia activity from an apartment across the street.

The story of the F.B.I. setting up a sting operation against the mob was portrayed in the popular movie *Donnie Brasco,* which was released in 1997. The movie starred Johnny Depp as Donnie Brasco, an undercover F.B.I. agent who infiltrated the mob for six years trying to bring down members of the Bonanno family of New York and the Santo Trafficante family of Tampa. Playing the role of mobster Lefty Ruggiero was Al Pacino. Other than the movie being set in Miami instead of Holiday, it was a fairly accurate portrayal of the F.B.I.'s operation at King's Court.

It all started when James Vincenzo Aquafredda, a low-level mobster in the Gambino Family, bought a Florida garbage company. Living in New Port Richey, he "squeezed" the other garbage companies with "association dues" and "initiation fees." When

Aquafredda opened a gambling parlor in a Port Richey apartment, it caught the attention of the F.B.I. None of this mob activity could happen without the blessing of Santo Trafficante. The plan was to lure the Bonanno family down to the New Port Richey area and bring down a host of crime families when they started doing business together. Operation COLDWATER, named after Aquafredda, was the F.B.I.'s best chance to bring the Mafia to its knees. The entire plan hinged on the abilities of F.B.I. agent Joe Pistone, a.k.a. Donnie Brasco to orchestrate the meeting of the powerful crime families at King's Court.

One of the families I brokered the Bonanno family into an alliance with was the Santo Trafficante family in Tampa, Florida. Among other crimes, the primary criminal conspiracy was that the two families became partners in illegal gambling and drug distribution at a private club called King's Court. It was in a big octagon building on five acres near Tampa. King's Court was equipped as an illegal gambling casino with craps tables, roulette wheels, and blackjack. What neither Mafia family knew was the fact that the King's Court club was set up by the F.B.I.

Joe Pistone, a.k.a. Donnie Brasco

The two top Mafia members from the Bonanno family, who Donnie Brasco lured down to Florida, were Lefty "Guns" Ruggiero and Dominick "Sonny Black" Napolitano. They were under the direction of Bonanno family boss Phillip "Rusty" Rastelli, who was serving time in a Pennsylvania prison. Sonny Black and Santo Trafficante made a business agreement at Pappas Restaurant in Tarpon Springs. The Kings Court was allowed to be operated by the New York Mafia as long as half the take went back to Trafficante. This was not a problem since the back room gambling business and the distribution of cocaine were bringing in enough money for both families.

To keep the operation running long enough for the F.B.I. to get all the evidence they needed to put away the mobsters for a long time, the undercover agents needed to pay off the local law enforcement.

Tony Rossi was able to find a crooked captain from the Pasco County Sheriff's Department. Captain Joseph Donahue, who lived in New Port Richey, took the Mafia bribe money to keep his men away from the King's Court. Yet the sting quickly came to an end. Even with Captain Donahue on the take, another group of deputies who were not on the take, found out about the King's Court and raided the place arresting all the mobsters present that night.

In all, sixty members of five different crime families were arrested on charges of illegal gambling, racketeering, robbery, drug dealing, extortion, and bribery. Although Santo Trafficante, the biggest fish of the group, was indicted, the feds didn't have enough evidence to convict him. The mob had a justice system of their own to punish the mistakes of their family members. Lefty Ruigerro was "sent for" to be executed by the mob. The F.B.I., who had the mob bugged, stepped in to save his life by arresting him, before the execution went down. The F.B.I. hoped that Lefty would be grateful and turn on his mob family, giving them the information they needed to convict other members of the Mafia. Lefty refused to snitch and was sentenced to twenty years in jail, of which he served eleven. Sonny Black was also "sent for" and killed by the mob. When the authorities found his body, they found his hands cut off. This was the Mafia's way to send a warning to other mob members to be careful who you introduce into the mob.

Sonny made the deadliest of all introductions when he introduced me to Santo Trafficante in Florida and I shook Trafficante's hand. It didn't matter that I had set the whole deal in motion with Trafficante regarding the gambling operation at King's Court. I could never have met a boss as powerful as Trafficante without a direct introduction from at least a capo (Sonny).

Joe Pistone, a.k.a. Donnie Brasco

The two New Port Richey accomplices with big roles in Operation Coldwater, Captain Joseph Donahue and King's Court owner Richard Milbauer, also met their deaths in suspicious ways.

Captain Donahue was found dead on his bathroom floor from a gunshot wound to his temple. Donahue had recently been indicted on racketeering charges having accepted money from the Mafia. He was preparing to appear in court where he was expected to testify against the mob and against members of the sheriff's department. Although the Pasco Sheriff Department quickly ruled Donahue's death a suicide, there were a lot of reasons to question that ruling. Primary among them was that Donahue's body was found in a posed position with his ankles crossed and both index fingers pointed at his chest. Another reason for doubt was that the crime scene may have been tampered with by deputies. Evidence was possibly thrown away, and the gun found next to the body was fired again by deputies before being put into an evidence bag.

In the case of Richard Milbauer, he was found shot to death with a hunting rifle. Pasco County Sheriff John Short ruled the death a suicide. Many local people doubted this story as well, because of the awkward use of a long hunting rifle instead of a pistol. Also, the fact that Milbauer, who walked with a limp, had polio which would have made it difficult for him to hold a rifle and shoot himself. The deaths of both Donahue and Milbauer were very suspicious given the mob involvement and the possible collusion of the Pasco County Sheriff department who investigated both cases.

The "Donnie Brasco" episode had all the elements of a Hollywood movie, thereby capturing the attention of the media and painting a disturbing picture of a seamy side of west Pasco County. But during the eighties and nineties the prevailing characterization of the New Port Richey area was not one of mobsters and dirty cops, rather one of general decay. No longer were the wealthy purchasing homes and spending their winters in the area. Other than the healthcare industry and the school system, the local economy was largely dependent on poor paying service industry jobs. Low incomes led to an increase in the crime index to the point where it was nearly double that of the country's average.

The New Port Richey downtown area was relatively quiet, with most retail businesses having moved to the bustling highway 19 corridor just blocks to the west. Sims Park, once a source of pride for the community, had been taken over by teenage gangs and vagrants who lurked in the shadows after dark. New Port Richey had started the 20th century with high hopes to be a destination for the famous and wealthy, then finished the century trying to stave off poverty and decadence.

The once grand Hacienda Hotel, a symbol of New Port Richey's opulence, operated as a community hotel from the 1950s through the 1980s. Instead of hosting wealthy aristocrats from New York, the hotel specialized in birthday parties and high school proms. One of the more interesting and unique acts that played at the Hacienda during this time was Tiny Tim. Born as Herbert Khaury, Tiny Tim somehow had gained recognition on Johnny Carson's Tonight Show by playing his ukulele and singing "Tiptoe Through the Tulips." He agreed to play the Hacienda, but showed up without any musical accompaniment. In a bind, the Hacienda tried to find him a band and contacted Locke Elementary music teacher and Richey Suncoast Bandleader Henry Fletcher.

Tiny Tim was a very peculiar man. As weird a person as I have ever met. I brought my trumpet to play with him the best I could. But it was rather difficult since he played everything by ear, and only in the key of C.

Henry Fletcher

The Hacienda stopped operating as a hotel after sixty years. In 1986 Governor Bob Graham dedicated the building to serve as a living facility for the needy in the New Port Richey area. Gulf Coast Jewish Family Services targeted abused and neglected children, impoverished elderly and people who struggled with mental illness. It remained a treatment facility until 2003, when the city of New Port Richey purchased the Hacienda for the gaudy price of 2.2 million dollars. The city hoped to preserve the hotel, which was officially listed on the National Register of Historic Places. Three years later, in the midst of another economic recession, the Hacienda was boarded up and left that way for the next ten years.

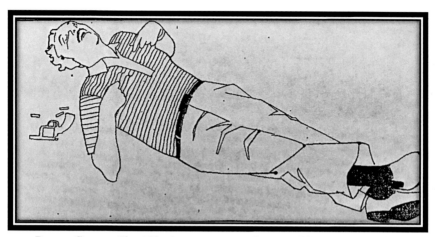

Pasco County Sheriff crime scene rendering of Deputy Donahue

King's Court, Building was moved to new location and is now a church.

Richard Milbauer

Richard Milbauer's father, Michael Milbauer
at his New Port Richey Office, formerly the
Port Richey Land Company office.

15

Revitalization

In the 1980s Dr. James Gills purchased thousands of acres southeast of New Port Richey from Jack Mitchell Jr. On the land, he relocated Trinity College, and began a large housing development project known as Trinity. With population growing in the area, Seven Springs Middle School opened its doors to students in 1996, followed by J.W. Mitchell High School, built on an adjoining lot four years later. A new shopping center named Mitchell Ranch, anchored by Publix and Target, was built nearby. In the same vicinity, brothers Trey and Frank Starkey developed a neo-traditional community called Longleaf, then designed and sold a 2,500 acre multi-use housing development named Starkey Ranch. The Trinity area was growing fast, bringing a higher income bracket to an area in need of the resources.

Few people knew that across from the Mitchell Ranch, on State Road 54, behind the ten-foot brick walls, lived a man who was on the Forbes top 400 Richest People in America list. Roy Speer was the co-founder with Bud Paxson of the Home Shopping Network based in St. Petersburg. He started his company almost by accident in the seventies. Speer's radio station WWQT had an advertising client who couldn't pay their bill. Instead of cash, they gave the station 112 electric can openers. The station put the can openers up for sale on their show *Suncoast Bargainers*. The show was a success and morphed into the Home Shopping Network when they purchased the Home Shopping Channel on local cable access. Besides HSN, Speer, a lawyer by trade, also spent time developing homes in Seven Springs.

The Trinity area is not technically part of the city of New Port Richey, but does have a New Port Richey mailing address and is generally referred to as New Port Richey. Yet unlike traditional new development suburbs of old cities, Trinity operates, not as a suburb of New Port Richey, but as a suburb of Tampa. Each day thousands of its residents make the roughly forty-minute commute down the Suncoast Parkway to Tampa businesses. Residents of Trinity rarely find the need to venture to the oft forgotten downtown of New Port Richey. Further exemplifying the move of both population and money from the old parts of New Port Richey to the new parts of Trinity, New Port Richey Community Hospital moved from its location near downtown to a new state of the art building in the heart of Trinity in 2012.

The New Port Richey area had been transformed from a playground for the rich and famous during the 1920s, to a retirement community in the 1960s, to a bedroom community going into the twenty first century. By the year 2000, only twenty percent of New Port Richey's residents were born in Florida. Western Pasco County had expanded its population largely due to the low cost of living combined with improvements in education, medical care, and sources of activity. Sheriff Chris Nocco has made more improvement in public safety than has been seen in years. Reduction in the city's drug, prostitution, and crime problems have given residents pride in the community once again. With safe neighborhoods, and increasingly younger families, a bedrock of any community, moving into the area. The median age of 44 in the year 2000, no longer reflected a retirement community, instead a growing community of families. The ten square mile area of New Port Richey, Elfers, and Trinity boasted a population of over 100,000 people in the year 2015.

In recent years there has been a bit of a renaissance, as interest has slowly grown about the unique history of New Port Richey. What was once old, is becoming new again. Over one hundred fifty years ago, The Hope family came to an area known as Hickory Hammock and mined the nearby springs for salt. The area soon became known as Hopeville. On March 16th, 2001, the State of Florida, dedicated the new Werner-Boyce Salt Springs State Park on the same land that the

Hope family mined salt for the Civil War. Members of the Hope family still live in the area. The park is just blocks away from the home of Vic and Jan Mallett. Vic is the great-grandson of James Washington Clark and Frances Louise Hope. Vic's great-grandfather was the settler who brought city namesake Aaron Richey here in the 1880s.

For years, people have been coming to our city because it was cheap to live here. But through it all, things have remained pretty much the same. The river is just as beautiful as it was when my family first settled here years ago, and good people continue to call the area home.

Vic Mallett

Enchantment Park along the Cotee River was a popular spot in a growing town that had just been named when they started their post office in 1915. One hundred years later, the City of New Port Richey had a grand reopening of their newly revamped Sims Park. The two million dollar facelift was a splendid success, attracting many residents back to the downtown area. The connection the citizens have with the park and the river can't be ignored.

Those waters run deep through my life as sure as the blood in my veins. I remember my first kiss was at Sims Park, where young lovers came to sit on the bank. I was smooth as Errol Flynn as I launched my boat into the moonlight while my true love waved goodbye from the shore.

Terry Kline, longtime resident

On the southeast end of the park, another reconstruction project is underway. The Hacienda Hotel is being restored to its original 1927 grandeur. First constructed to be a beacon to illustrious northerners as their winter home, the Hacienda is being positioned to return that same quality of attraction back to the once thriving streets of downtown New Port Richey. On the northeast end of the park, the West Pasco

Historical Society continues to preserve the area's illustrious past and make connections to its promising future.

The Chasco Fiesta is still going strong. It has operated for seventy consecutive years and its boat parade, starting back in 1922, is the oldest in Florida. The event has become a big fundraiser for nonprofit organizations. In 2015 twenty-five non-profits raised a combined total over $200,000. More than a quarter of a million people attend the Chasco Fiesta each year, bringing in millions of dollars to the local economy. Another tradition from the past that can be seen each Christmas is the giant wooden Christmas cards placed around Orange Lake. The Dutch Colony from Holland, Michigan, started a colony in New Port Richey known as Little Holland and brought with them the custom of displaying wooden Christmas cards each holiday season.

Another key component to the revitalization of New Port Richey lay in a couple housing projects. Started in 2004, prior to the housing bubble bursting, Main Street Landing sat dormant for ten years while the economy recovered. Now back on course, the complex will feature ninety apartment units overlooking the Cotee River. Another upscale apartment complex will occupy the former site of the First Baptist Church on Orange Lake. One of the city's most prominent developers, Frank Starkey, is leading the project that will bring another eighty-five high quality apartments to the downtown area. Starkey, a lifelong resident of the area, has a keen eye for urban development and sees a lot of potential for downtown New Port Richey capturing the attention of millennials, which would be integral for any sort of revitalization.

New Port Richey is a wonderful town. It has a great traditional street network, authenticity, outstanding natural and recreational amenities, a convenient location, and a beautiful setting. The center of town is particularly enchanting with its intact central business district, beautiful Pithlachascotee River,

140

Sims Park and Orange Lake, historic buildings including the landmark Hacienda Hotel, and convenient close-in neighborhoods. New Port Richey contains a rare combination of attributes that other towns covet and new suburbs can only dream of.

Frank Starkey

Both the residences at Orange Lake, to be named *The Central*, and *Main Street Landing* will maintain the historical identity of the downtown neighborhood homes and buildings in their architecture. Many of the buildings from the era of the 1920s are still intact in the downtown area. When US 19 was constructed and traffic was diverted around downtown New Port Richey, the inadvertent outcome was that the downtown of the 1920s was preserved from typical urban sprawl. In prototypical evolution of cities, the buildings of the past are often torn down to make way for modern shopping centers, thereby robbing the community of its historical character. New Port Richey has been largely ignored by modern expansion, leaving the rich culture of its past still alive in the old buildings left standing.

Among the original 1920s buildings still standing and in use downtown are three buildings on the intersection of Main Street and Grand Boulevard. The original Port Richey Land Company Building, the original First State Bank and the original Clark Building are all occupied by new businesses. Of the three, the Land Company, which was the first brick building in town, is the closest to its original form of when it was built in 1919. There are ten other buildings built downtown during the 1920s, all still in use, and many of them in the same architectural style of the Hacienda. The old Thomas Meighan Theatre has been converted from showing movies to live theater. There had been additions made to the building but the original structure remains. The Richey Suncoast Theatre harkens back to the time when the Thomas Meighan Theatre was the pride of New Port Richey. In addition, two historical buildings were added to the downtown area when they were moved to Sims Park. The old Seven Springs Schoolhouse is now the home of the West Pasco Historical

Society and the old Our Lady Queen of Peace Church is now a city building called Peace Hall.

Many of the homes from the glory days, both around town and along the river can still be seen. The small bungalow home of George and Marjorie Sims, that hosted so many movie stars, is the first house next to Sims Park. The home of Gerben Devries, the founder of the Chasco Fiesta, is just up the hill on Central Avenue. The little home on the corner of Grand Boulevard and Illinois Avenue hasn't changed much since a twelve-year-old boy named Jim Irwin once lived there.

It's along the Pithlachascotee River that the stars shine the brightest. Johnny Cash and June Carter's home still looks out over the river across from Miller's bayou. Just a couple doors down is Aunt Martha Oelsner's place where the mound made by the Tocobaga Indians one thousand years earlier is still preserved. Up-river a bit headed towards the downtown area are the homes of the affluent development of Jasmin Point. There is nothing left of the golf course accept a small pond which undoubtedly contains some 1920s Wilson golf balls submerged on the bottom. The street names read like a who's who of New Port Richey's glamorous past. There's Meighan Court, Burns Point Circle, and Avery Road.

There are a few houses that remain intact along the river. Most notable is the former home of James Becker, the auto manufacturer and co-developer of Jasmin Point. Made with the same pink stucco design as the Hacienda, the home stands out to those meandering down the Cotee River. Years after Becker owned the house, the aunt of Shirley Temple lived there and was said to have been visited by her famous niece. The home of Becker's partner in numerous New Port Richey projects, Warren Burns, had fallen in disrepair and was demolished. The only thing left behind of the property is the old carriage house and stable. Other homes still standing nearby include the houses of golfer, Gene Sarazen and perfume mogul, William Loveland. The Sarazen house is the only house not directly on the river, but instead located across the street on the site of the old golf course. The house of his neighbor and friend, Thomas Meighan, is gone except for part of the property wall, a pool house and a scaled down version of the pool. All these homes from the glory days of the 1920s are located in the same area along a bend in the Cotee River about a half mile north of downtown.

From 2004 to 2007 a series of five murals were painted on the sides of buildings in the downtown area of New Port Richey. One is of the Henry-Grey stilt house. Another is a re-creation of a 1920s Cotee River swimming picture, using the faces of current residents. The other three depict scenes at the Hacienda and downtown streets with famous celebrities such as Babe Ruth, Gloria Swanson, Charlie Chaplin, and Mary Pickford. Some portions of the paintings are historically accurate while others are based more on local legends and lore. It's entirely possible that Ruth, Swanson, Chaplin, and Pickford never set foot in New Port Richey. What is certain however, is that Meighan, Sarazen, Wynn, Hitchcock, Cameron, Errol, Greenwood, Cash, Irwin and dozens of other celebrities did spend time in New Port Richey. The mystery and intrigue of who was or wasn't here only adds to the city's mystique and allure.

The connection that New Port Richey has with its past days of fame and fortune lies in the memories along every street and around every corner. The same downtown buildings that the celebrities of the twenties walked by are the same buildings citizens walk by today. The numerous stories of famous people walking these streets, some true, some just rumors, help make up the splendid tapestry of the city's remarkable history. For a few short years during the Roaring Twenties, New Port Richey was a destination for some of the nation's most wealthy and famous people. The stock market crash of 1929 took away that dream of being the Hollywood of the East, but nothing can wipe away the memories of New Port Richey's *glory days.*

Former Thomas Meighan Theatre now Richey Suncoast Theatre.

Former Seven Springs School, now home to West Pasco Historical Society.

Orange Lake 2016.

Redeveloped Sims Park.

Celebrities who visited New Port Richey during the Glory Days (1920s & 30s)

According to newspaper accounts, and stories both present and past.

George Ade - Author, Pulitzer Prize winning columnist. Member Jasmin Point Golf Club

Irvin Bacheller - Journalist, writer. Involvement in Arcade Building on Main Street.

Harry Bannister - Theater and movie actor.

Richard Barthelmess - Academy Award nominee best actor. Bought land in New Port Richey.

Rex Beach - Author, screenwriter.

James Becker - Owned Elmore Motor Company. Bought home and invested in New Port Richey.

Earl Benham - Costume designer, actor. Bought large tracts of land in New Port Richey.

Ralph Brewster - Governor of Maine, US Senator.

Donald Brian - Actor, Dancer, Singer.

William Jennings Bryan - Orator, politician.

Nathan Burkan - Charlie Chaplin's lawyer. Part of Syndicate to own land in New Port Richey.

Warren Burns - Industrialist. Bought home and invested heavily in New Port Richey.

Irving Bush - Multimillionaire businessman.

Madeline Cameron - Theater and movie star.

Frank Case - Author, owner of New York's Algonquin Hotel.

Edythe Chapman - Theater and silent movie star.

Al Ciuci - Professional golfer.

Irvin Cobb - Sports writer.

Richard Conover - Professional tennis player. Bought home and retired in New Port Richey.

Wellington Cross - Actor, Bought land in New Port Richey.

Frank Crowinshield - Editor of *Vanity Fair.*

Dorothy Dalton - Silent movie star.

Clarrence Darrow - Famous attorney.

Robert Davis - Author, owner New York Sun.

Arthur Deagon - Comedian, actor.

Billy DeBeck - Popular syndicated cartoonist. *Snuffy Smith.*

Walter Donaldson - Famous song writer.

Leon Errol - Movie star, comedian. Bought land in New Port Richey

George Fawcett - Actor

William Gaxton - Vaudeville actor, movie star, married to Madeline Cameron.

Charlotte Greenwood - Actress. Bought land in New Port Richey. Played Aunt Eller in *Oklahoma.*

Clark Griffith - Hall of Fame Baseball Player, owner Washington Senators.

Ann Harding - Theater and Movie Star.

Sam Harris - Theater owner / Movie producer. Bought land in New Port Richey.

August Heckscher - Multimillionaire philanthropist.

Ray Hitchcock - Actor. Bought land in New Port Richey.

Victor Heerman - Actor. Part of syndicate to own land in New Port Richey.

Cecil Holland - Actor, make-up artist.

Edna Hopper - Silent film actress.

J.C. Huffman - Theater director.

Frances Ingram - Famous opera star.

Henry King - Film director.

Bohumir Kryl - World renowned big band leader.

Hal Lanigan - Editor Great Neck Newspaper.

Ring Lardner - Famed sports columnist Chicago Tribune.

Jesse Lasky – Founder of Paramount Pictures.

Marcus Loew - Owner Loews Theaters and MGM studios.

William H. Loveland - Owner William Loveland Perfume Company. Owned a home on the Cotee River.

Charles Maigne - Film director, screenwriter.

Christine Mangasarian - Actress. Wife of Earl Benham. Frequent visitor with sister Flora Zabelle.

Riccardo Martin - Famous opera tenor.

John McCormick - Movie producer.

Thomas Meighan - Movie star. Built home in New Port Richey.

Robert Montgomery - Owner of Westchester Independent Newspaper in Boston.

James Neill - Theater and silent movie actor.

Grantland Rice - Famed sportswriter, sports reel producer.

Blanche Ring - Actress / singer. Bought land in New Port Richey.

Frances Ring - Actress. Wife of Thomas Meighan.

Stanley Robinson - All-American football player, coach. Owned a garage in New Port Richey

William Robinson - Famous gardener, journalist. Bought a house in New Port Richey.

Joseph Santly - Dancer, actor. Bought land in New Port Richey.

Gene Sarazen - World class golfer. Built home in New Port Richey

Ivy Sawyer - Cabaret dancer, singer. Bought land in New Port Richey.

Edgar Selwyn - Broadway producer. Bought land in New Port Richey.

Nicholas Schenk - Owner MGM Studios

Oscar Shaw - Theater and movie actor, singer.

Charles Torrey Simpson - Famous botanist and author.

Ernest Truex - Theater, movie, and television actor.

Lupe Velez - Theater and Movie Actress.

Thomas Watson – Alexander Graham Bell's assistant.

W.J. Wells - General Manager of Macy's.

Charles Winniger - Theater and movie actor.

Ed Wynn - Comedian, Emmy Award winning actor. Owned Palm Theatre in New Port Richey.

Flora Zabelle - Actress. Bought land in New Port Richey. Lived in Hacienda Hotel for extended time.

Rumored but not substantiated.

Irvin Berlin - Song writer, God Bless America, Easter Parade, White Christmas. Bought land in Bay Shore Estates

Al Capone - Gangster. Seen in nearby Tarpon Springs.

Charlie Chaplin - His attorney did stay at the Hacienda.

Lillian Gish - Possible stay at Moon Lake Ranch with sister Dorothy.

Alfred Hitchcock - Possibly visiting friend in New Port Richey.

Joseph Kennedy - Possible stay at Moon Lake Gardens.

Mary Pickford - Stated she had not been to New Port Richey in a letter to Ralph Bellwood .

Babe Ruth - Baseball star. Fished in Aripeka and Hudson. Friends with Sarazen. Possible stop in New Port Richey for beer.

Gloria Swanson - Actress. Owned land in New Port Richey. Announced visit to city did not materialize.

Shirley Temple - Child movie star possibly visited Aunt in New Port Richey.

Lana Turner - Actress. May have been at Moon Lake as a 16 year old budding star.

Paul Whiteman - Famous big band conductor. Invested in land in New Port Richey. Possible opening act at Moon Lake Ranch.

Celebrities in New Port Richey after the Glory Years

Joe Biden – Vice President of the United States.

George W. Bush – President of the United States.

Jimmy Carter – President of the United States.

June Carter Cash – Singer, Country Music Hall of Fame.

Johnny Cash – Singer / songwriter. One of best-selling musicians of all time. Owned home on Sunset Boulevard in Port Richey.

Billy Graham – Evangelical television Minister.

James Irwin – Astronaut, Apollo 15. Lived on Grand Avenue at age eleven. Went to local schools.

Sarah Palin – Politician.

Ronald Reagan – President of the United States.

Tiny Tim – Entertainer who performed in Hacienda.

Frank E. Smith – Author, wrote under alias Jennifer Hale. Lived 25 years in New Port Richey.

Roy Speer - Owner of Home Shopping Network. Lived in New Port Richey off State Road 54.

Dan Quayle – Vice President of the United States.

Selected Readings

Avery, Elroy M. *The Genesis of New Port Richey.* New Port Richey, Florida: Avery Library and   Historical Society, 1924.

Bellwood, Ralph. *Tales of West Pasco.* Hudson, Florida: Makovec Printing, 1962.

Cannon, Jeff. *Then and Now, New Port Richey.* Charleston, South Carolina: Arcadia Publishing, 2011.

Carozza, Adam J. *Images of America, New Port Richey.* Charleston, South Carolina: Arcadia Publishing, 2004.

Carozza, Adam J. *New Port Richey: Myth and history of a city built on enchantment.* Tampa, Florida: University of South Florida, Scholar Commons, 2009.

Crosby, Genevieve. *Celebrating Community: Tarpon Springs,   Reflections on 125 Years.* Tarpon Springs, Florida: City of   Tarpon   Springs, 2013.

Dill, Glen. *The Suncoast Past.* New Port Richey, Florida: The Suncoast News, New Port Richey Chronicle, 1987.

Doll, Susan, and David Morrow. *Florida on Film.* Gainesville, Florida: University Press of Florida, 2007.

DeVries, Gerben M. *Chasco, Queen of the Calusas.* New Port Richey, Florida: New Port Richey Press, 1922.

Drye, Willie. *For Sale, American Paradise.* Guilford, Connecticut: Rowman & Littlefield, 2016.

Grant, Hayter-Menzies. *Charlotte Greenwood, The life and Career of   the Comic Star of Vaudeville, Radio and Film.* Jefferson,   North Carolina: McFarland &Company, Inc. 2007

Horgan, James, and Hall, Alice, and Hermann, Edward. *The Historic Places of Pasco County.* Dade City, Florida: Pasco   County Historical Preservation Committee, 1992.

Hooker, Rob and Brackett, Ron. *Tampa Bay Through The Times.* Gainesville, Florida: Seaside Publishing Inc. 2008.

Irwin, James B. *To Rule the Night, The Discovery Voyage of Astronaut Jim Irwin,* Philadelphia, Pennsylvania: A.J. Holman Company, 1973.

Kite-Powell, Rodney, and Elizabeth Laramie Dunham. *Brief History of Hillsborough County, Florida:* Tampa Bay History Center

MacManus, Elizabeth, and Susan MacManus. *Citrus, Sawmills, Critters, Crackers.* Tampa, Florida: The University of Tampa Press, 1998.

McCarthy, Kevin M. *The Book Lover's Guide to Florida.* Sarasota, Florida: Pineapple Press, 1992.

McMorrow-Hernandez, Joshua. *Tampa Bay Landmarks and Destinations.* Charleston, South Carolina: Arcadia Publishing, 2015.

Obenreder, Julie J. *West Pasco's Heritage.* New Port Richey, Florida: West Pasco Historical Society, 1974.

Pistone, Joseph, and Brandt, Charles. *Donnie Brasco, Unfinished Business.* Philadelphia, Pennsylvania: Running Press, 2007.

Revels, Tracy J. *Sunshine Paradise, A History of Florida Tourism.* Gainesville, Florida: University Press of Florida, 2011.

Sarazen, Gene, and Wind, Herbert. *Thirty Years of Championship Golf.* Classics of Golf, Ailsa, Inc. Stamford, Connecticut, 1987.

Starkey, Jay. *Jay Starkey's Things I Remember.* Brooksville, Florida: Southwest Florida Water Management District, 1980.

Stevenson Ash, Pauline. *Florida Cracker Days in West Pasco County 1830-1982.* New Port Richey, Florida: West Pasco County Historical Society, 1985.

Stronge, William B. *The Sunshine Economy,* Gainesville, Florida: University Press of Florida, 2008.

Swanson, Gloria. *Swanson on Swanson.* New York, New York: Random House, 1980.

Tash, Paul. *Tampa Bay, Through the Times,* St. Petersburg Times. Canada: Pediment Publishing, 2008.

Turner, Gregg M. *The Florida Land Boom of the 1920s.* Jefferson, North Carolina: McFarland & Company, Inc. Publishers, 2015.

Wynn, Nick. *Tin Can Tourists in Florida 1900-1970.* Charleston, South Carolina: Arcadia Publishing, 1999.

1930 New Port Richey Telephone Directory

List of Telephone Subscribers, New Port Richey Exchange
Including Elfers and Hudson

CORRECTED TO DECEMBER 1, 1930

A

Anderson Dean W r Massachusetts av.39-Black
Atkinson William r Cent & Jefferson .. 67-Red
Atkinson William farm............36-Black
Avery Dr Elroy M r Dixie Hghwy. 67-Black

B

Bailey M L r Port Richey..........72-Black
Baillie P J r Gunn Highway..........88-Red
Barnett Chas W r Dixie Highway.......49
Battin Horace M r Kenwood av.... 69-Green
Becker James H r Jasmine Point.....74-Black
Bentley Ruth D r Missouri & Dixie Hghwy 27
Blum E C r Old Grove............64-Black
Brewton W H atty Dixie Highway..... 75
Brewton W H r Dixie Hghwy 100
Burnette-Patterson Lumber Co Missouri av..58
Burns J J r Jasmine Point.............53
Burns Warren E r Jasmine Point........54
Burns-Becker Corp rl est Miss & D Hghwy.91

C

Campbell E P r Elfers..............88-Blue
Case Mrs Carrie M r Circle 83
Chaddock R E r Old Port Richey.... 20-Blue
Chamberlain A gro Elfers.......88-Green
City Hall Dixie Highway..............14
Clark D H r Port Richey 70-Red
Clark James r Dixie Highway......30-Green
Cooper C J r Georgia & Jackson 64-Green
Cooper Service Station Dixie highway......76
Critchley W H r Illinois...... 61

D

Dane Carl J r Main........... 98-Blue
DeWoody Chas r Washington & Mass 67-Green
Dingus Henry W r Montana av.......5-Blue

E

Elfers Pay Station Elfers..................0
Emerson G D r River dr N.............28

F

Felix Father r Washington 78
First State Bank Main & Dixie.........22
Florida Power Corp Dixie hwy......23
Foley Mrs J J r Jasmine Point........77-Red
Fralick R W r Dixie hwy...........63-Red

Frissell Mrs W J Sr r Van Buren......81-Blue
Fugazzi Pinellas Groves r Elfers....... 4-Blue
Fullington M A r Massachusetts av..39-Green

G

Gulf High School New Port Richey....41-Red
Gulf Springs Lodge Hudson..............0
Gurney Mrs J W r Indiana av.......51-Green

H

H & S Motor Co Dixie Highway.........44
Hacienda Hotel Riverside Pl & Sims Pk . ★18
Hancock Dr W S r The Circle.........26
Hancock Dr W S Jr Dixie Highway.....26
Harris W J r Trouble Creek rd.......36-Blue
Heinnickel H J plumber Elfers.......85-Black
Herms Charles F r Dixie Highway....67-Blue
Herms Oscar W Dixie Highway..........31
Hoffman Chas N Jr r Delaware av....63-Blue
Holbrook George r Riverside Dr S.......87
Holmes M A r Madison...........85-Blue
Holtzscheiter John G r Dixie Highway.71-Green
Hyams Isabell F r Old Grove............93

J

Jackson J S r Riverside Drive N....77-Black
Jahn W K r Dixie Highway........32
Justamere Inn Main 24-Black

K

Kaley Mrs E W r Indiana av..........94
Kelley G B r Van Buren...........81-Black
Knowles William r Hudson.........65-Red

L

Lapham Mrs Clyde r Virginia..........72-Red
Leigh Owen S r Dixie Highway.....36-Green
Lockard J C r Main...............86
Lohnes G H r The Old Grove.........43
Loveland Wm r Jasmine Point..........47

M

Manning Mrs E M r Delaware..........50
McDowell James r Dixie Hwy......71-Black
Meeth Louis H r Gulf High Drive 79
Mitchell J M real estate Elfers......40-Green
Mitchell J M r Elfers.............40-Red
Moe A L r Sunset Point............69-Black

N

Nelson Capt John r River dr......20-Black
New Port Richey Hotel Dixie Highway.....0

New Port Richey Press Main...........60
New Port Richey Public Market
Dixie Highway 90
Nunn Arthur M r Kenwood av......72-Green

O

Oelsner Mrs Dora r River dr.....20-Green
Olson August r Massachusetts av......92-Blue

P

Pembrook's Cleaning & Laundry
E Mississippi av...................96
Phillips W H Grocery & Mkt
Dixie Highway 16
Police Dept Dixie Highway............55
Poole Hoffman Drug Co Dixie Highway....11
Poole Lockard Service Sta Dixie Hghwy..25
Port Richey Co rl est Main & Dixie Hghwy.57

R

Reagan I W r Elfers...........88-Black
Remington H W r Dixie Highway.......35
Riviere Rev C A r Pennsylvania a.....51-Red
Rothera H S r Missouri av......37

S

Sarazen Gene r Jasmine Point...........27
Sarment J r Virginia av.........51-Black
Sass Fred r Manor Hotel bl......70-Black
Scofield E P r Water...........41-Black
Seaboard Air Line Railway Dixie Hghwy 12-Blue
Shaw Fred A r Palm Haven 42-Black
Sims George R r Dixie Highway........62
Smallwood J H r Hudson.....65-Green 2-Rings
Smith Nellie M r Indiana av..........97
Stulting Mrs C J r Congress........92-Black

T

Thorp Charles r Dixie Highway.........95
Twitchell Service Station Elfers.......38

V

Vahey's Pharmacy Dixie Highway........99

W

West Fla Bond & Mtg Co Dixie Highway..91
Western Union Dixie Highway..........89
Wilkes Edward Y Sr..........Main-46
Williams J L r Elfers............4-Red
Wright Edgar A r Dixie hwy 30-Red

SEE PAGES FOLLOWING CLASSIFIED DIRECTORY FOR NUMBERS IN NEARBY CITIES

154

ON FLORIDA'S WEST COAST

ON FLORIDA'S WEST COAST

HACIENDA HACIENDA
HOTEL
NEW PORT RICHEY, Florida

HACIENDA
HOTEL
NEW PORT RICHEY, Florida

New Port Richey is especially well located for visitors coming into Florida by automobile . . . , being on U. S. Highway No. 19 (Fla. 210) which is the through short route south from Brooksville. Excellent highways open up exciting sight-seeing to you in all directions. Famous Moon Lake Gardens and Dude Ranch are only 9 miles from the Hacienda Hotel. New Port Richey is largely a resort community and you will see here many beautiful winter homes of prominent persons.

We invite you to come and enjoy with us this fine atmosphere of friendly hospitality and comfort; and whether you stay one day, a week or the entire season the same pleasing service is at your disposal.

AMERICAN PLAN

Rates begin at $5 daily, single.
$9 daily, double.

Weekly and seasonal rates on application.

GRAY HOLMES - ROBERT HOLMES, Jr.

Owners-Managers

156

A Hotel Whose Friendly Hospitality Will Please You

View of the Lobby Through to the Dining Room

Views of the Cotee River from Hotel Grounds

The Patio and Part of the Shady Hotel Lawn

THIS is an invitation to you to come and visit the Hacienda Hotel at New Port Richey, Florida, ... a friendly hotel, open November 15th to April 15th, which offers every conceivable modern comfort and convenience in an atmosphere of such charm and beauty that, once experienced, you will want to come again and again.

The Hacienda Hotel is one of the most beautiful smaller resort hotels in the Sunshine State . . . . . . authentically Spanish in architecture and richness of appointments . . . . located on the banks of the tropical Cotee River . . . . with fifty guest rooms, each with private bath, solid carpeted floors, steam heat, telephones and available with either twin or double beds. Guest rooms are available singly or in combination en suite with sun parlors.

From your first glimpse of the Hacienda Hotel you will find an ever-increasing array of features appealing to your sense of beauty, your love for comfort, enjoyable environment and hospitality. You will delight in the true tropical splendor of the spacious grounds comprising acres of grassy lawns studded with shrubbery, palms and flowers. You will love the wide terraces, the arched doorways, the inviting balconies and the large patio.

You will find a new sense of luxury, relaxation and comfort in the big lobby with its massive open fireplace, with its large doorways opening on the terrace on one side and the cloister on the other. Hacienda Hotel service is planned to anticipate, inobstrusively, your every need for comfort and entertainment whether you come to rest or to enjoy outdoor sports and recreations.

The dining room of the Hacienda Hotel enjoys a splendid reputation along the west coast of Florida. A cuisine of variety, freshness and goodness tempts your appetite for every meal.

Outdoor sports have always attracted Hacienda guests. The Cotee River bordering the grounds offers some of Florida's finest fresh and salt water fishing. It is only two miles from the hotel dock to the open Gulf of Mexico and the hotel maintains a 28-foot launch as well as small boats for the use of guests. Within the hotel grounds are shuffle-board courts, putting greens and tennis courts. Only a few miles away is the Tarpon Springs golf course and within 30 to 45 minutes drive from the hotel are Tampa, Clearwater and St. Petersburg with all their numerous attractions.

Index

158

159

161

Author with First Family of Port Richey

Author Brian Schmit with Frances Clark Mallett, granddaughter of New Port Richey pioneers James W. Clark and Frances Hope Clark, her husband Walter Mallett and son Vic Mallett.

Other books by Brian Schmit

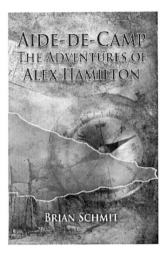

Aid-de-Camp, The Adventures of Alex Hamilton

There are few historical figures that were more important to the creation of America than Alexander Hamilton. In Aide-de-Camp: The Adventures of Alex Hamilton the author takes the reader on an exciting journey by asking the question, What if the rumors were true? History comes alive in dramatic fashion when one of our greatest stories is told with an entertaining twist.

A Friend of America

This fast-paced story takes the reader on an adventurous trip to colonial Boston. Seventeen-year-old Alexander Hamilton joins his buddy Hercules Mulligan on a quest to save the Sons of Liberty! Along the way, they meet Boston patriots Samuel Adams, John Hancock, Ben Edes, John Adams and Paul Revere. A Friend of America is historical fiction at its finest. Intended for use in the middle school classroom